TRANSFORM YOURSELF THROUGH FOOD

KITCHEN*Alchemy*

ANN BOWEN-JONES
& PHILLIPPA LEE

**Spirituality
&Health**
BOOKS

Copyright © 2010 by Ann Bowen-Jones and Phillippa Lee
Photography copyright © 2010 by Thomas Kachadurian

Spirituality & Health Books
129 1/2 East Front Street
Traverse City, MI 49684
www.spiritualityhealthbooks.com

Cover and interior design by Sandra Salamony

ISBN: 978-0-9818708-6-1

Printed in China
First Printing, 2010
10 9 8 7 6 5 4 3 2 1

Dedication

It is our great joy to dedicate this book to Phillippa's sister Caroline, and to the food-loving women of Ann's family — her mother Morfudd, her maternal grandmother Jane Ann, her Aunt Beryl, sister Carol and niece Siwan.

We dedicate it also to our readers, all of you out there whom we may never meet but with whom we feel a kinship. We sense we are part of a body of people who are transforming their lives from the inside out, day by day, by bringing love and attention to cooking, eating and sharing the precious gifts of the earth — food.

contents

cooking as alchemy 39

SOUPS 45

beauty & meaning 59

starters 65

SHOPPING 81

main DISHes 87

RHythm 107

vitality sauces¹¹³

healing₁₂₇

sweets¹³³

INtRODUCtION

FEEDING THE SPIRIT

There is so much that is wonderful about food today. More people than ever before are taking an interest in what they eat and where it comes from, and organic food has suddenly become mainstream. We are at a moment of such exciting fusions of cuisines and approaches, and the pace of innovation is exhilarating.

There is also, however, unprecedented anxiety, guilt and uncertainty around what we eat. The combined pressures to eat well while living impossibly demanding lives, to work out what "well" actually means among the plethora of conflicting advice, to try to be slim in the midst of constantly bewitching temptation, ensure that many of us are unhealthily obsessed with food. And too many of us have simply given up or given in.

But it really leaps out to us that one of the things we may have overlooked as a culture is that we are spiritual beings as well as physical bodies. As our bodies need food for survival, so our souls can starve without wisdom and beauty. Fortunately, there are tremendous sources of both available to guide us, from different traditions, the inspiration of the cosmos and the natural world, to that of cultures which have elevated their relationship to food and nurturance to connect with transcendent truths — think of French cuisine and yoga's subtle philosophy of body-mind dynamics. Most importantly, there is our own inner wisdom, emanating both from our intuitive connection to Source and from our instinctive animal nature.

We believe that we can benefit from a different lens through which to look at food, re-imagining the relationship between food and spirit at every stage of the journey from sourcing to eating.

Alchemy provides one such perspective. It is a philosophy which has woven a tantalizing and mysterious thread through the ages. Alchemy has transcended boundaries of geography, culture and religion to appear in many and varied civilizations as diverse as those of Egypt, China, Persia and Greece.

At alchemy's core is transformation, with the transmutation of base into gold being a potent metaphor for enlightenment. Food is, essentially, transformed by cooking to render it more palatable and nutritious. It metamorphoses again when eaten and its individual components become part of our bodies. We suggest that our consciousness can also be transformed through each and every interaction with food. Through becoming more deliberate about how and what we eat, we can become more alive, more peaceful, more connected.

Love is the most potent transformative ingredient of all. In our heart of hearts, most of us would agree that the solution to so many of our challenges is to bring more love to bear. When love, this deepest dimension of life, is restored to its central place, clarity arises and tension is relieved. It is a core belief of ours that this is no whimsicality or wishful thinking, but rather a highly pragmatic guiding principle. When applied to food, the consequences of, for instance, loving our planet more (and therefore respecting all that grows on it), or of loving ourselves more (and therefore really nurturing ourselves as we eat) are truly incalculable. We can all become kitchen alchemists, transforming our tables by choosing the ingredients of love.

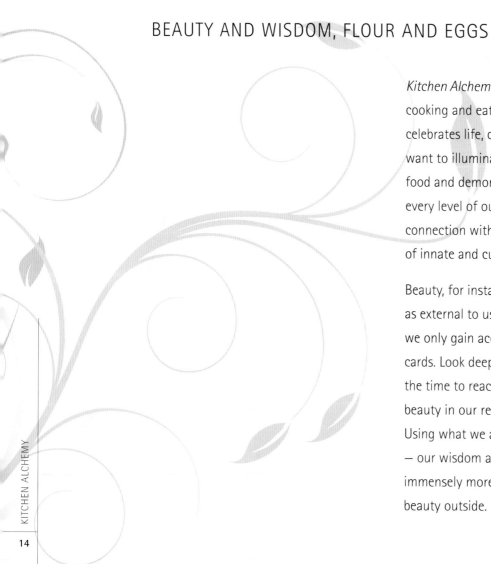

BEAUTY AND WISDOM, FLOUR AND EGGS

Kitchen Alchemy approaches shopping, cooking and eating food in a way that celebrates life, creativity and beauty. We want to illuminate our relationships with food and demonstrate how food can heal every level of our being by restoring the connection with these ever-fresh springs of innate and cultural wisdom.

Beauty, for instance, is so often presented as external to us, something privileged we only gain access to through our credit cards. Look deeper and we find that taking the time to reach within will create simple beauty in our relationship with food. Using what we already have in our lives — our wisdom and experience — can be immensely more satisfying than seeking beauty outside.

When we cook, we assemble ingredients which are ordinary, prosaic perhaps, or at least taken for granted, like flour, milk, eggs, cheese, some salt, maybe some sugar. We use others which especially please us, like pomegranate and coconut, cashew and chili oil. The simple and sometimes slightly quirky combinations result in utterly delicious food to suit differing moods and needs — hearty or delicate, plain or fanciful. We are always seeking that alchemical marriage made in heaven!

We all have to eat, so it is empowering to realize that every time we fulfill that fundamental need we have choices which may seem small in themselves, but which cumulatively can quite simply transform our lives.

Ann Bowen-Jones
& Phillippa Lee

ABOUT THIS BOOK

We are fascinated by what we see reflected in the media and in our families and friends concerning food, eating and health, and we are immersed in finding our own paths through the contemporary paradoxes of thin/rich, nurturing/independent, healthy/forbidden. The recipes and accompanying essays then, are as fragments of a crystal, each refracting the light to cast a different perspective on this complex topic. Truly, we adore food in all its myriad aspects. Our interests, therefore, fuse the psychological and the spiritual, the cultural and the anthropological, the sensory and the delightfully greedy, plus the sober issues of well-being, both personal and global.

The recipes included here all have certain qualities:

They reflect our own eating habits — mostly vegetarian or vegan with an occasional meal of fish and poultry.

More importantly, these recipes awaken our taste buds through intense and surprising flavors. Richness of flavor beguiles us to be fully present to what we are eating, to truly appreciate each mouthful. Our food may be simply prepared — which indeed is a virtue in our busy daily lives — but depth of flavor inspires our brains to register the act of eating to the fullest degree. This awareness results in smaller quantities of food feeling both more fulfilling and more filling. We believe that eating deliberately can transform food into an elixir that both nourishes and heals.

We do not seek to give advice about what you should or shouldn't do differently — you have enough of that already. Rather, we want you to explore shifts in seeing that may have the power to seep imperceptibly into your life.

NOTE ON INGREDIENTS

In the making of this book, we engaged in a cross-Atlantic adventure, our American editor and photographer initiating us into an alternative, Alice in Wonderland world of food names, meanings and measurements. We now feel decidedly more sophisticated, enlightened and perhaps just a little bemused by the unexpected similarities and differences.

So, for your benefit and interest here are some translations that relate to our book:

in England, a biscuit is a cookie
chips / french fries
coriander leaves / cilantro
cornflour / cornstarch
courgette / zucchini
cos lettuce / romaine lettuce
digestive biscuits / graham crackers
double cream / heavy cream
single cream / half and half
greaseproof paper / wax paper
icing / frosting
maize / corn
tart / pie

All the measurements have been painstakingly converted and tested for both American and European kitchens.

We hope that *Kitchen Alchemy* inspires you to re-imagine your own relationship to food, and that the ideas and images gravitate towards you at the perfect time to encourage you on your journey. This book comes to you with love, and it would make us very happy if even a little of the joy of life that this project has brought us could communicate itself to you.

why eat?

MEETING TRUE NEEDS WHEN WE EAT

Our thoughts and feelings have so much more influence upon our reality than we realize. For example, when people of normal weight eat a large amount of food, they rarely put on extra weight. In contrast, many overweight people have "only to look at an éclair" for their weight to pile on. Metabolism and its set-point are big factors, of course, but might it be also the subtle programming power of belief?

We've never forgotten a shiatsu therapist telling us that addiction arises from not giving ourselves the nourishment of what we really need. So much of the time we are way out of touch with our real needs, or we quickly suppress them as being inappropriate, forbidden or inexpedient.

We believe that it's okay, even more, that it's natural and healthy to trust our feelings, our intuition, our bodies, ourselves. In fact, re-learning to trust, with the effortlessness of the child we once were, is a doorway to finding fulfillment in so many areas of life.

Giving Yourself What You Need

If you're truly hungry, take a moment to connect with your body and appetite to discover what you'd really like.

Do you crave something savory or sweet?

Crunchy or creamy?

Chewy or soft?

Do you need food to give you a boost of energy or to calm you down?

Do you want something warming or chilling, liquid or filling?

Keep on asking questions until you've honed in on the food which would most fully meet your need. Imagine yourself in a process of divination, sensing the energetic imprints and emanations of the foods and matching them to your own energy.

Now, give yourself that food — or, of course, the closest kind available. Nothing is out of bounds. Make the dish for yourself and put it on a beautiful plate, then sit down and eat with complete awareness and appreciation.

Eat s-l-o-w-l-y. Savor the layers of flavor and experience the changing textures in your mouth as you chew. Imagine the goodness and energy flooding through your body. Give yourself as much as you want — yes, really! But while you're eating, tune in to your feelings of satisfaction and fullness, as these are your friends and guides. Notice the signals of satiety, subtle at first. Learn to trust yourself and let your body guide your eating.

Now that you've finished, ask yourself if you feel you've really eaten, really received nourishment. Has the food satisfied your body and your spirit? Do you feel a warmth spreading from your belly throughout your body? Do you feel an alertness, a new readiness for what you need to do next? Do you feel calm?

This is a good way to develop your body's capacity to instinctively self-select foods for health. Although your needs may change according to the sway of weather, hormones and metabolism, you can tune into subtle signals for guidance, listening to the feelings constellating in your body. By taking a moment to focus inward, you can

In a life of busyness, creating the space to eat alone in stillness can be a revelation, while eating with others in true communion can be an enormous source of strength.

learn to distinguish between a temporary high and a sustained feeling of well-being by simply noticing what is going on while you eat and the food's effects during the next few hours. Counterintuitively, it has been found that taking the time to eat in this way, mindfully, actually saves time and energy. The meal becomes a spiritual practice when you're too busy to meditate. Eating is a doorway to connecting with the perspective of your soul.

Studies of naturally thin people show that they tend to eat whatever they fancy, whenever they feel hungry, and stop as soon as they've had enough. They are in touch with their natural appetites and preferences and therefore what their particular metabolisms and lifestyles need. It is less of a head-trip, and certainly not a guilt-trip.

WHY DO WE EAT?

When we asked ourselves and others why we eat, we found responses like:

for a treat
for a reward
for comfort
hardly ever out of hunger
I see the food so then I want it
I don't love myself so I eat crap food
I see the food advertised
for fuel
often I don't realize I'm snacking
social pressure
to please my mother/ lover/ friends
to spite myself
to fill the void
because I feel emotional
because it's there
if I don't eat, I'll die
I can't control myself

Since we all have to eat, why not use food as a means to bring into our lives the things we long for?

Gather together your thoughts and senses and approach your food gently, with affirmations such as these:

I eat to heal myself.
I eat to restore balance in my life.
I eat to bring a sense of peace to my day.
I eat to deepen my appreciation of myself.
I eat to invite the sacred to reveal itself
   in my life.
I eat to expand time.
I eat to guide my life with joy.
I eat in order to remember who I really am.

As a first act of faith, try eating something delicious, right now, very, very slowly. As a coach I increasingly encourage people to move away from planning how they want to be, way off in the future. Rather, I ask them to bring into their lives the qualities they most desire just for the next five minutes. And then, perhaps, the next five minutes, and the next. Each few minutes of peace can add up to a lifetime, as the present moment is all we have. And, the more we cultivate a quality, even if it's only for a few minutes at first, the more we draw the quality toward us and spot opportunities for its cultivation. —AB-J

saLaDs

POUR COMMENCER

Take 1 green pepper and 2 tomatoes
and cut them into rings and hearts. Mix those
with olives, black olives, and go for a swim
in a green sea with her (or him).
Then serve your salad on two bellies. Pour
a little sun-warmed olive oil in your
salt navel, some vinegar in hers
(or his), and eat slowly with your fingers.
Empty the bottle. Open a second. Then
lick your plates. You will need them again.

— JON STALLWORTHY

LITTLE GEM, WATERCRESS, AVOCADO AND GRIDDLED HALOUMI SALAD WITH LEMON CAPER DRESSING

A vibrant, sense-enhancing salad that makes a great dinner party starter. It is very easy to prepare and the different textures and tastes complement each other wonderfully.

SERVES 2

half a little gem lettuce

2 handfuls watercress

1 ripe avocado

2 quarter-inch slices haloumi cheese

¼ cup / 50 milliliters best olive oil

half lemon

2 tablespoons / 25 grams capers

pinch sugar

Wipe haloumi cheese with a kitchen towel to remove excess water.

Heat griddle pan and cook haloumi on each side until golden brown.

Shred little gem lettuce and divide between 2 plates.

Place washed watercress on top.

Halve and peel avocado, cut into slices and arrange on top of salad.

Put haloumi on top of avocado to make a nicely heaped arrangement.

FOR THE DRESSING: Whisk olive oil with squeezed lemon juice, add a pinch of sugar, pepper to taste and the capers.

Pour dressing over salad and serve while haloumi is still warm.

HERB, WALNUT AND QUINOA TABOULI SALAD

It is now official — quinoa is a wonder food. It is actually a herb seed and contains a balanced combination of amino acids, making it a protein in its own right. What the books don't say about quinoa is that it's a wonderfully well-behaved protein. Just dry roast it for a minute, then add boiling water and cook until every grain appears to wear a halo — these are, in fact, little spiral threads that come apart from the main grain. Once cooked it can be used like rice or couscous. It is light in taste and texture with a slight crunch and has the ability to absorb other flavors without disintegrating.

We love to use quinoa in this sense-awakening tabouli salad. The finished dish is refreshing, healthy and a beautifully vibrant green.

SERVES 4

1 cup / 140 grams quinoa

small bunch each of mint,
flat leaf parsley and cilantro /
fresh coriander

1 bunch spring onions

half pint / punnet cherry tomatoes

1 Lebanese cucumber*

¼ cup / 100 grams walnuts,
toasted

2 lemons

¼ cup / 50 milliliters extra
virgin olive oil

* LEBANESE CUCUMBERS *are smaller
than the Dutch or English type. They are
more readily available than they used to
be and have a more intense flavor than the
larger cucumbers. If you can't find them,
use half an English one.*

Dry roast and cook the quinoa in 4 cups / 800 milliliters water for 10 minutes. Cool. Place in large salad bowl.

Finely chop herbs and toss with quinoa.

Wash and finely chop spring onions, add to dish.

Halve the cucumber, remove seeds and finely dice flesh leaving the skin on. Add to dish.

Cut the tomatoes into quarters and add to the rest of the ingredients with the toasted walnuts.

FOR THE DRESSING: Squeeze lemon juice into a separate bowl and whisk with olive oil and a pinch of salt. Pour the dressing over the salad and toss well.

selecting the ingredients of Life

Most of us have encountered fruit that was so ripe, so bursting with life and color and flavor, that it was utterly irresistible. I treasure the memory of a Spanish fig tree whose fruit drew me so strongly that I returned to its bounty again and again, vying with the thousands of rather aggressive wasps who were equally captivated.

As you shop — be it at a market stall or a supermarket — take a moment to practice tuning into the vitality of the produce you select. We often do this unconsciously, reaching for what is freshest, for what seems to say to us, "Buy me!"

While what you are drawn to may not be the most perfect-looking fruit or vegetable in the array, it may just be the one which *connects you perfectly* with the sunlight its cells have captured and transformed through trillions of biochemical reactions. That sunlight — energy — is present in the fruit in a condensed form, and the energy is ready to be absorbed into your cells when you eat the fruit.

Most people can develop the ability to sense the life-energy in food, it just takes a little practice. Notice the larger-than-life quality of misshapen tomatoes in a farmers' market, picked that morning perhaps, and compare them with their anemic supermarket equivalents, as regular as eggs in plastic boxes. Which of them reminds you most of lazy, sun-soaked Greek afternoons? —AB-J

Rachel's apple

This is the experience of a friend of ours who, in the most ordinary of circumstances, connected deeply with the radiance in her food.

As a manager in Oxford, each day I sat down in my well-ordered office and did an easy job. On one particular morning, my mind was roving over the matter of nutrition and how I might eat myself healthy. I'd invested in a fruit bowl for the office, but that was as far as I had got, and I was pretty reluctant to actually eat any of it. I munched at my

organic apple, in front of my computer, idly wondering, "What good are you?"

Then I looked at the apple. It was shimmering. Really. It looked so juicy. I could see every cell. The fruit was milky white, shining and radiant, and energy seemed to pour out of it, surrounding my hand and moving in and out of its skin. I looked closer, trying to absorb what I was seeing. The apple was alive!

And, it looked delicious. I could easily see that having this vibrantly powerful food in my stomach, radiating out to each part of me, would be an incredible advantage. I got a clear instinct that each of my cells might behave and look just like this, given the right treatment. The apple seemed to be made out of light; it was sparkling. I was holding it in my hand, and it felt like part of me. I realize now that where it had just been an apple to eat, now I was relating with it, having asked the question, "What good are you?"

Food is alive for me now. Simple as that. I know now how we work together to create more energy and support each other. And, remember, this happened while I was sitting in an office at a desk in Oxford, taking a break from handing out timetables for the next week's training sessions.

ROASTED PEAR, SMOKED DUCK AND FRISÉE SALAD
WITH TOASTED WALNUTS AND CITRUS HONEY DRESSING

This salad was created while on a writing retreat in southern Scotland.
The sun was shining, the words wouldn't come and the local smokehouse was
too close to ignore. The result of a morning outing was this smoky, tingly salad.

SERVES 2

1 smoked duck's breast*

2 pears

half a head curly endive/frisée lettuce

¼ cup / 50 grams walnuts, toasted

1 grapefruit

1 lemon

1 teaspoon honey

1 teaspoon grain mustard

6 tablespoons olive oil

1 tablespoon walnut oil

Peel, core and cut pears in half and place in a small saucepan. Drizzle with olive oil.

Zest the grapefruit and sprinkle on pears. Cook for 25 minutes on medium heat until soft.

On one plate, arrange the shredded frisée, the duck breast cut into strips and 2 pieces of pear. Sprinkle walnuts on top.

FOR THE DRESSING: Mix olive oil, walnut oil, mustard, squeezed grapefruit and lemon in a bowl or jar. Pour over salad.

*An alternative to
DUCK BREAST would be
either smoked chicken or
good smoked cheese.

PARISIAN SALAD

This salad is one of my all-time favorites. Its implausible combination of flavors works stunningly well. I first ate it in the leafy courtyard of a tiny restaurant in Paris, hot and weary from arduous shopping and much in need of sustenance! This dish nourished my soul and revived me to continue my explorations. —AB-J

Combine:

mixed salad leaves

chopped dried figs

cumin seeds

chunks of goat's cheese

good vinaigrette

Accompany with interesting bread, the best butter and a glass of chilled white wine.

STICKY ROAST ARTICHOKE, GARLIC AND ORANGE SALAD
WITH POMEGRANATE AND RED WINE DRESSING

I am a fan of Brighton Grove. Not the south coast, but the west end of Newcastle upon Tyne where there lives a fabulous Asian store — an emporium filled with all the food that I love to shop for, cook with and eat.

Here is where I buy sumac, homemade vegetable somosas, Lebanese cucumbers, boxes of ripe alfonsa mangoes and my favorite — pomegranate molasses. This is a dark, rich, Middle Eastern syrup made purely of Persephone's fruit. It is wonderful dribbled on creamy soups and added to eggplant tagines. In this salad it lifts tinned artichokes to a whole new level. —PL

1 jar artichoke hearts, in brine

1 head garlic

1 orange, half for juice, half peeled and segmented

²/₃ cup / 150 milliliters olive oil

³/₄ cup / 175 milliliters pomegranate molasses

³/₄ cup / 175 milliliters red wine

2 tablespoons balsamic vinegar

salad leaves, a good mix with watercress and rocket

croutons (optional)

Preheat oven to 400F / 200C.

Drain artichoke hearts and squeeze each to extract any water. Place in roasting pan with a drizzle of olive oil. Add whole cloves of garlic leaving the skin on. Roast for 10 minutes.

Add ¼ cup / 50 milliliters pomegranate molasses and red wine. Roast for a further 20 minutes, turning over the artichoke hearts halfway through cooking. At the end of cooking, the hearts should be slightly sticky, caramelized, and with a reddish color. The garlic cloves should be soft and sweet.

FOR THE DRESSING: Pour any juices left in roasting pan in a glass screw-top jar. Add olive oil, the juice from half the orange, balsamic vinegar and the rest of the pomegranate molasses. Shake well and season to taste.

TO SERVE: On two plates, arrange salad leaves, artichoke hearts, garlic cloves and orange segments. Pour the dressing over the salad.

HOT SWIRLED SALADS

It's early January, that still point of the year. We think particularly of the Thai Theravadin and Tibetan Buddhist monks who take the whole of January as a time of seclusion. Those of us living very much in the world may also want to attune to nature's cycles: the somber beauty of a muted palate of earthy browns, greys and dark reds. The response of our own bodies to the seasons may bring about a desire to hibernate, to luxuriate in that still point.

A slightly paradoxical way of eating is called for to support us at this time. Not simply the heart-warming homely soups, stews and casseroles of mid-winter, but also the crispy, light-green shoots and leaves of spring which are starting to appear in some places. Interestingly, Chinese medicine advises that all food be heated at this time of year, however briefly.

Inspired by this, and feeling its rightness for our bodies, we devised these dishes in which contrasting salad ingredients and more substantial elements are swirled together in a very hot wok for no more than 30 seconds. This takes the chill and energy-dampening qualities out of the fresh food, and simultaneously gives us an intriguing blend of warm tastes and textures.

Try adapting your usual favorite salads. Experiment!

Sow peas and wild garlic for foraging in a month or two: those tiny shoots come up early!

Here's one combination:

In a wok, over low heat, dry-roast a handful of walnuts or pecans. Stir regularly until they start to brown and smell appealing.

Turn up the heat and add a drizzle of olive oil. Stir in quickly a bunch of watercress and chopped fresh pear. Swirl for 30 seconds. Remove from heat and add Stilton or other good blue cheese. Add the fresh juice of a lemon to taste.

And another:

Swirl mixed green leaves, chopped spring onions, and cherry tomatoes in olive oil. Remove from heat and add shaved Parmesan and red wine vinegar.

And another:

Dry roast pumpkin, sunflower and sesame seeds.

Add olive oil and swirl quartered little gem lettuces with endive, spinach, rocket or virtually any green. Remove from heat and add chunks of goat's cheese. Sprinkle with balsamic vinegar.

COOKING as aLCHEMY

COOKING HAS ALWAYS BEEN ABOUT TRANSFORMATION

Cooking renders edible and nutritious our raw materials — our potatoes, legumes and root vegetables. Nuts and grains release their hidden stores of aromatic nourishment in the heat of our ovens and stovetops.

Cooking makes the mundane magical. Flour and butter and milk are transformed into an airy cake that pleasures the eye and the tongue, bonding the giver and the recipient. Cooking celebrates our special events and builds community.

Cooking brings both variety and constancy into our lives as corn becomes tortillas, chowder or cornflakes according to a country's culture and climate. Recreating familiar foods from basic elements strengthens group

identity and reassures and comforts us. The power of our own creativity helps us rise above entrenched traditions.

When first beginning to cook, humans lacked a highly developed sense of self or a clear impression of how their bodies looked (mirrors are a fairly recent invention!). In sharp contrast, we now live in a culture of transformation, but of transformation often motivated by self-obsession and hatred of ourselves. No aspect of our lives is untouched — we scrutinize our body's shape and weight, our skin, our hair, our psyche and our behavior — the armies of personal trainers, coaches and therapists are testament to our mania.

Although we are fixated with cookbooks, reality gastroporn and the latest diet, we cook less and less. Watching TV chefs, we eat packaged dinners on our laps. There is a begrudging and unacknowledged resentment of the time cooking takes co-existing alongside the fantasy recipes we will make one mythical day when things are finally under control and we have plenty of free time.

But what if the selection, preparation and eating of food became a source of intimate space, inner peace and connection to the world around us?

Think about it: for many of us, shopping, preparing and eating a meal may be the only opportunities in the whole day to do something for ourselves and our loved ones.

Why not transform our kitchens into oases?

Why not bring more awareness to our cooking?

Who knows, it may stimulate a re-think of the possibilities in our lives. We may find ourselves transformed.

Cooking is an activity that has the potential to evoke in us deep peace or immense stress. The reality is that most of us have to cook something every day for ourselves or our families, and that reality can sometimes feel like a burden.

Surely we have all experienced the sense of freedom while on holiday: eating in restaurants, being waited on by others — careless of shopping or making choices about meals.

And yet . . . at home . . . .

We believe that our state of mind while cooking has a profound effect on the food we produce.

At home, in our kitchens, we should remember that what we do makes an enormous difference to us and those for whom we cook. Our kitchens can be refuges where cooking becomes a tool for happiness.

a few slow, deep breaths and allow any stressful thoughts to fade away as you make a shift from where you have been to where you are now.

If cooking from a recipe book, get familiar with the instructions. Read through them a couple of times and check that you have everything you need. This may sound simplistic, but it will stop the cries of distress in the middle of, say, cake-making, when you realize you've forgotten the lining paper or you remember that you lent your cake tin to a neighbor.

take a moment to really look at them. Notice the colors, the combination of textures, the sheer abundance. This is an opportunity to be present, to really appreciate the beauty of food and the magic that is about to happen.

Now take a moment to honor and acknowledge yourself, your family, the food and the process that is life and your connection to it. Make the preparation of food the most important act of your day.

SOUPS

MMMMM....

This is the sound we make when we sense the potential delight in an aspect of the world, reach out to it, bring it towards us, and experience its essence as intense pleasure or beauty.

I remember a supremely happy meal shared with Beth, a friend's daughter. She was at the time perhaps four years old. Every mouthful of the entire meal was accompanied by long, loud and intense mmmm's. At first from Beth alone, and then from both of us!

Little children's appetite for sensual pleasure and their utter freedom in its expression are all the more poignant for so quickly giving way to mechanical fork-lifting of un-tasted food while channel-surfing for adrenalin-fixes or anaesthesia. How on earth to translate that prolonged childish joy in the simple to our complex and often jaded adult selves?

Make each meal, whether we are feeding ourselves or others, whether erotically or tenderly, an opportunity to harvest joy; to calm our busy lives, to send well-being and energy to our cells and our surroundings. These "mmmm" moments of serendipitous meditation may be the only moments of presence or peace in the day. Let us appreciate and multiply them so that their influence spreads beyond the moment and affects the way we go about the rest of our lives.

—AB-J

CARROT, CELERY ROOT AND COCONUT SOUP

A creamy, truly irresistible soup. You can give it a bit of bite by adding a drizzle of chili oil at the end, or for a touch of tartness add a swirl of pomegranate molasses.

SERVES 4

2 tablespoons olive oil

1 white onion

3 cups / 450 grams carrots

3 cups / 450 grams celery root/celeriac

1 tablespoon vegetable stock powder

1 teaspoon salt

1 14-ounce tin coconut milk

small bunch cilantro/fresh coriander

Heat olive oil over medium-low in a medium-sized soup pot.

Peel onion, cut into small chunks and add to the hot oil.

Peel carrots, cut into small chunks and add to pan.

Peel celery root/celeriac, cut into small chunks and add to pan.

Sauté the vegetables until just lightly brown.

Pour in enough hot water to just cover the vegetables. Stir in the stock powder, add the salt and bring to a boil. Turn down the heat and simmer gently until cooked.

Remove from the heat and, using a hand blender, blend soup until creamy. Add coconut milk.

Lastly, chop cilantro/fresh coriander and stir through soup.

Everything you create is unique precisely because you are making it. Your soup will be different from my soup even though we use the exact same ingredients and the exact same recipe. It will be different because we each have innate qualities that show up in small but distinct ways, like how vegetables are chopped and how soup is stirred.

SPINACH AND SORREL SOUP

A spring green soup bursting with energy and health.

4 tablespoons butter

1 white onion

6 cloves garlic

1 potato

4 cups / 1 liter vegetable stock

2 large bags fresh spinach

¼ cup / 50 grams sorrel leaves

2 tablespoons half and half /
single cream (optional)

Melt butter in a large soup pot.

Peel and chop onion and garlic. Sauté in butter for 5 minutes over medium-low heat.

Peel and finely dice potato and add to the pot. Continue to cook for a further 5 minutes.

Add stock and bring to a boil. Simmer until the potato is cooked.

Wash spinach and sorrel and add to the soup, cooking for a further
5 minutes. With a hand blender, blend ingredients together until smooth.

If soup seems too thick, add a little water. Adding cream will make a richer finish.

fifteen minutes of fame in the life of a fruit

A comedian once talked about his frustration with pears: They sat in his fruit bowl for weeks, hard as rocks. He kept creeping up to them and giving them a sneaky prod to see whether they were ready to eat. *No, not yet... No, not this time either... Still not ripe... Ah, well, they should be soon....*

However, the next time he looked, the fruit had become soft, mushy, tasteless. The comedian felt as though the over-ripe pears were taunting him. *Ha, ha you missed us! We were ripe – for fifteen minutes – and you blew it!*

Exaggerated (only slightly!) as this is, the truth is that everything has its moment in the limelight, everything has its peak of perfection. To embrace transience and truly tune into the ripeness of a fruit, for example, leads us to favor the flavor of seasonality over the year-round availability of tasteless facsimiles.

The gifts the seasons give us are more poetically described by André Gide:

Bunches of grapes hang from strings in front of a sunny bay; each grape meditates and ripens, secretly ruminating light: it elaborates a perfumed sugar.

In his paean to opening to pleasure, *Fruits of the Earth*, Gide goes on to say that if we are not sufficiently amazed at being alive, we are not sufficiently awake to the joys that are possible within our daily activities. Our culture, with its emphasis on the metrics of nutrition, weight and health can easily overshadow the value derived from simply enjoying the moment without measuring it. Just as it can be said that a prayer of the heart grows out of a particular moment in time and cannot be said the next day – for that day will have its own prayers – so we can be guided by the cycles of the produce we gather to us.

CHICKEN, BARLEY AND CORIANDER BROTH

SERVES 4

We call this "a clean soup." It feels very nourishing and light, and the coriander gives it a fragrant freshness. This soup is wonderful made with leftover chicken.

2 leeks

1 white onion

2 large carrots

2 sticks celery

2 tablespoons olive oil

leftover roast chicken carcass or 2 chicken thighs (skin removed)

2 teaspoons ground coriander

1/4 cup / 50 grams pearl barley, rinsed

4 cups / 1 liter good quality vegetable stock

1 cup dry white wine

Trim the top and bottom of leeks. Cut in half, wash and slice thinly.

Peel onion, carrots, celery and cut into small pieces.

In a medium-sized soup pot, heat oil over medium-low. Add vegetables and gently sauté until coated in oil and very lightly colored.

Add chicken, coriander and barley.

Sauté for a few more minutes, then add vegetable stock and wine. Bring to a boil, then lower the heat and simmer for 45 minutes. During cooking remove any scum that makes its way to the surface and stir occasionally.

Remove carcass or thigh bones, return meat to the pot.

Add more water to make a lighter soup.

See the Lemon Roast Chicken recipe on page 105.

SOUPS

LENTIL AND MUSHROOM SOUP WITH GOAT'S CHEESE CROUTONS

I used to live in the wilds of Northumbria, in a cottage at the top of a hill with no electricity and no road. There was a wood-fueled stove to cook on and my partner would gather logs from the local woods and carry them up the hill on his back. On autumn mornings we would get up early and, two fields along, gather newly sprouted field mushrooms for breakfast, saving some for this wonderfully intense soup. Served with a green leaf and hazelnut salad, this recipe makes a filling and satisfying meal. —PL

SERVES 4

FOR THE SOUP:

¼ cup / 50 grams butter

4 tablespoons peanut / ground nut oil, or other general purpose cooking oil

¾ cup / 175 grams French puy lentils, rinsed*

1 white onion

2 leeks

2 sticks celery

5 cloves garlic

1 pound / 500 grams field or portabello mushrooms

4 cups / 1 liter vegetable stock

½ cup / 125 milliliters white wine

1 lemon

handful flatleaf parsley

FOR THE CROUTONS:

ciabatta bread

1 teaspoon olive oil

1 garlic clove

3½ ounces / 100 grams goat's cheese

lemon

In a medium-sized soup pot, gently heat butter and oil together over medium-low.

Finely chop onion, leek and celery. Add to pan and sauté until lightly colored.

Peel garlic and crush; add to vegetables.

Chop mushrooms into rough dice and add to pan. Sauté for a further 5 minutes.

Add lentils, vegetable stock and white wine. Bring to boil, then turn down heat and simmer for about 40 minutes, or until the lentils are cooked.

While the soup is simmering, thinly slice the bread and rub with a little olive oil and the edge of a garlic clove. Arrange on a baking sheet and place in a 400F / 200C oven until crisp. Remove and crumble or spread goat's cheese on top of the slices. Return to the oven until the cheese begins to melt.

TO SERVE: Taste and adjust seasonings in the soup. A squeeze of lemon at the end enlivens the flavors. Ladle soup into bowls, sprinkle with parsley and float a crouton on top of each.

These LENTILS are brown, so they complement the colors of the mushrooms. They're worth seeking out as they have a beautiful earthy flavor and retain their shape when cooked.

CReATIVITY IN THe KITCHEN

Trust yourself. Knowing nothing about food preparation is a wonderful foundation for creativity. If you don't know what is supposed to go together, you have the potential for outrageous experimentation. The geniuses of this world are great because they choose to think outside the cookbook.

Think of a meal as a painting: have a red day with radicchio, cherry tomatoes, roasted garlic and rare tuna. Be neutral with creamy mash potatoes, roast parsnips and a chickpea and olive tapenade. Think green and cook up a springy soup with all the fresh vegetables you can find – finish it with a parsley and pistachio pesto.

Creativity is the excitement and magic of making something new, of playing, of bringing the unmanifest into unique and individual form.

Go to the cupboard and let a herb or spice be seen, or simply reach in and take the first jar that jumps into your hand.

Take one vegetable and cook it in different ways. See and taste the difference between broccoli that is steamed, stir-fried or baked in the oven. Which do you prefer?

Add layers and depth by adding ingredients such as soy sauce or almonds.

Taste the food as you go along. It's the best way to know what your taste buds like and will help the under-confident believe in their capacity for creative play.

We believe that food responds to a creative mind. One day carrots like to be matchsticks; another day, robust round coins. Ask the onions how they wish to be cut and let the answer be there in your hands.

Beauty & meaning

EATING MEANING

The physical form we see and touch is only part of what we take into ourselves when we buy and eat food. The flavor, texture, weight, history and perfume of food nourishes our spirits as well as our bodies. Food also affirms our cultural identity, our place in and familiarity with the world. Our choice of morning coffee and croissants, or bubble and squeak, or black beans and raw onion or pickled fish describe the circumference of our tastes neatly on a plate.

However adventurous our tastes later in the day, most of us need reassurance from the first meal, as we re-create ourselves anew from the dreamy and amorphous states of sleep. Rituals such as a cup of tea taken back to bed first thing in the morning, or a French lunch spanning three hours, give us a framework of constancy, a zone of stability, from which we gather the strength to surf the chaos of our lives.

Food has so many layers of meaning, both helpful and unhelpful. Most times it acts as a kind of social glue, bonding people together and symbolizing love and care. On the other hand, some foods can mean danger — the taboos against certain common foods have meant starvation amidst abundance, throwing the subjectivity of the term "food" into sharp relief. And to someone attempting to resume normal eating habits after a disciplined diet, food may seem frightening — something, like fire, not to be trusted and which could easily burst out of control. The Canadian psychotherapist Marion Woodman describes how, in a food binge, the specifically chosen food assumes an almost mystical significance as we, consciously or otherwise, commune with ice cream or chips or chocolate to change our condition and free a part of ourselves kept in denial. This denial frequently fuels the cycles of de-tox and re-tox which are now common parlance among women.

The deeply personal webs of connection we have consciously and unconsciously woven since we first looked into our mother's eyes play the profoundest role in shaping our identity. These connections are a cause for marvelling, and for celebrating by giving full rein to the diversity and creativity of our appetites for food.

The beauty in the light of someone's eyes, in a gesture; beauty in the silhouetted angle of leaf and branch, a sweeping grey cityscape, a tiny crystal of salt.

more it shows itself in the most ordinary of circumstances. It will stop us in our tracks, mainlining the divine like a bolt of lightning.

Food can be a potent source of beauty and, therefore, of quite literally coming back to our senses. The perfection of the raw ingredients, the light by which we eat and the way we eat can please us like fine sculpture and painting. In Paris, food is often seen as a form of art, a valued aspect of the culture on a par with, say, music. Watch a woman improvise a meal from the morning market's freshest ingredients; look at the way restaurant menus are composed and the courses orchestrated. The appreciation and pleasure in eating as a means of enriching daily life goes far beyond simply refuelling the body.

BEAUTY FUEL

True nourishment, or quality, subverts the need for mere quantity. With true nourishment, true satisfaction becomes possible. Influenced by this approach, we experimented with giving ourselves the foods we adored when we were trying to lose weight. We chose the greatest variety of textures and flavors, and whenever possible, the time to eat them oh — so — slowly. Our aim was to harvest the highest possible quotient of pleasure from each and every calorie. To our amazement, there was no upper limit to the joy of eating while slimming. All of which proves to us that beauty, that most intangible of dimensions, has powerfully practical benefits.

Here's a list of rainbow colors and their corresponding foods and nutrients:

- **Deep red to pale yellow:** carrots, sweet potatoes, pumpkins and cantaloupe contain the antioxidant carotene, but so do thyme, cilantro and parsley.

Nutritionists now talk about getting a rainbow of foods in our diets each day. Imagine a platter of mango, cantaloupe, banana, watermelon, green papaya and avocado, all drizzled with lime juice. This is a seriously enticing way to enhance health — feasting the eyes can be a wonderful guide to feasting the body on the variety of nutrients it needs.

- **Red, purple and blue to almost black:** these essential phytochemicals can be found in peppers, apples, cherries, grapes, eggplant/aubergines and oranges.

- **Dark-green** leafy vegetables like kale, chard, spinach, collard and bok choy are packed with important nutrients, which include the critical omega-3 fatty acids. Most people eating typical Western diets are deficient in these acids that help build strong cells and regulate inflammation.

- **White** vegetables also play an essential part in good health. Onions and garlic supply allicin, a natural antibiotic, which is thought to boost the immune system, fight heart disease, and reduce the risk of cancer.

- **Brown:** Selenium is an antioxidant and important for the well-being of the thyroid system. Foods high in this element include fish, seafood, animal products, most nuts and all legumes and cereals.

starters

A RADIANT ENCOUNTER

Sitting in a train station café on a rainy day in February.

A woman with white hair walks in, pushing her elderly father in a wheelchair.

They order tea and jam-filled Victoria sandwiches, oozing with fresh cream.

The daughter lovingly feeds her father bit by bit, sip by sip, her care for him evident in every delicate gesture and her soft smile.

He cannot talk but closes his eyes, puts his head back and allows the food to transport him.

His face is radiant with delight.

He looks like an angel.

Finished now, the daughter puts his scarf back on her father and they go out into the cold damp air.   —PL

CALENDULA CORNBREAD WITH CRÈME FRAICHE AND CORIANDER AND GREEN PEPPER SALSA

SERVES 4

Flower cookery is a passion of mine. It started at Confirmation as a small Catholic girl. As well as receiving a new name, I got a silver cross, black patent shoes and freesias in my hair. The priest came over as we sat at the Confirmation breakfast, and praised my flowers. In my young mind, food, flowers and the pleasure of praise became linked. Later, I indulged this love of flowers in home economics classes by making cakes and decorating them with violets, rose petals and lavender.

Here, I've used a basic cornbread recipe, then added chilies, red pepper and calendula flowers for a hot, red, golden-yellow look. The calendula is not essential but adds a greenish flavor. And the cake-like texture of the cornbread combines well with the tart creamy crème fraiche and smooth avocado. The salsa adds a crunch and freshness to the dish.

This is a good dish for a crowd. Carry the cornbread straight from the oven to the table and everyone tuck in. –PL

FOR THE SALSA

1 green pepper

6 green/spring onions

half bunch cilantro/fresh coriander

2 limes

4 tablespoons olive oil

Cut the pepper into a small, fine dice.

Wash and trim the spring onions, then shred finely.

Chop the cilantro/coriander finely.

Add everything to a bowl. Squeeze in the limes and add olive oil. Mix well.

FOR THE CORNBREAD

¼ cup / 55 grams butter, melted

1 cup / 250 milliliters natural yogurt

½ cup / 125 milliliters milk

2 eggs, beaten

1 cup / 130 grams cornmeal

4 heaped tablespoons / 55 grams all purpose flour

1 tablespoon baking powder

pinch baking soda

1 teaspoon sugar

seasoning

2 red chilies, deseeded and chopped finely

1 red pepper, deseeded and chopped finely

petals from 5 calendula flowers*, washed well

4 heaped tablespoons crème fraiche

2 small avocados

Mixing soda breads is a bit like making pancakes or scones — you hardly want the ingredients to touch. Just when you think you haven't mixed enough, you probably have.

*CALENDULA FLOWERS have been used as a medicine, dye and decoration for hundreds of years. Commonly, they are used to add color to salads, less well known is that their extract is often added to chicken feed to produce darker yolks.

Preheat oven to 350F / 180C.

Grease and line with parchment / grease-proof paper an 8-inch / 1.5 liter loaf tin.

Mix all the liquid ingredients in one bowl and all the dry in another.

Fold the wet into the dry very lightly.

Place the tin in the oven and bake for about 30 minutes. It's ready when the top is golden and a skewer comes out clean.

TO SERVE: Peel the avocados, cut into thin slices and arrange on a platter. Cut the cornbread into 4 inch-thick slices. Serve with crème fraiche, the salsa and avocado.

ARTICHOKE HEART PATÉ WITH TARRAGON, SUN-DRIED TOMATOES AND RICOTTA

We think of this dish as a basic cupboard paté. It takes minutes to whip together in a food processor and always tastes intriguing.

SERVES 4

1 9-ounce / 280-gram jar or tin artichoke hearts in oil*

1 12-ounce / 350-gram package or jar sun-dried tomatoes (drained)

7 ounces / 180 grams ricotta cheese*

2 tablespoons / 25 grams French tarragon

*For this recipe, we prefer ARTICHOKE HEARTS that have been marinated in oil as this gives the finished dish a more rounded flavor.

Drain the artichokes.

Strip tarragon leaves from stalk.

Place the artichoke hearts, ricotta, tarragon leaves and sun-dried tomatoes in the bowl of a food processor and mix well.

Taste and add seasoning.

Spoon into ramekins and chill for at least 20 minutes.

Serve with toasted sourdough bread.

*RICOTTA is a cheese that tends to hold flavors very well, but you could also try mascarpone or perhaps a creamy garlic Boursin.

MARINATED GOAT'S CHEESE

This recipe makes wonderful picnic food.

You will need several portions of goat's cheese, each marinated for a few hours in one of the following:

1 drop each of pure lavender and orange aroma oils, mixed with a couple of tablespoons of neutral oil such as sunflower

thyme, rosemary and chopped sun-blushed tomatoes in olive oil*

crushed garlic, torn basil leaves and olive oil

walnut oil and chopped walnuts

sumac, mint and olive oil*

SUN-BLUSHED TOMATOES *are semi-dried, therefore sweeter and less chewy. Generally packed in olive oil, you can find them in specialty groceries.*

Serve the selections with crispy French bread and unsalted butter.

Coming from the Arabic SUMMAQ, this is not the plant growing wild in North American gardens. Used as an enhancer, like salt, it is common in Middle Eastern cookery. Find it in your specialty grocery.

SWEET POTATO, CORIANDER, CASHEW AND LIME FILO PASTRIES

SERVES 2

These pastries make an exciting package of flavor and texture and do well served with the green pepper salsa from the **Calendula Cornbread** recipe (page 66). They make great party food and are also an elegant starter for a dinner party.

1 package filo pastry*

3 tablespoons sunflower oil

3 tablespoons grated fresh ginger

1 large sweet potato

¼ cup / 50 grams creamed coconut, grated*

¼ cup / 50 grams cilantro/fresh coriander

¼ cup / 50 grams cashews, toasted

1 lime

1 lemon

¼ cup / 50 grams butter

handful black onion seeds/nigella

Preheat oven to 350F / 180C.

Peel and cut the sweet potato into small cubes.

In a large frying pan, cook the sweet potato over medium-low heat in the sunflower oil until soft. Add the grated ginger and cook for a couple minutes more. Set aside to cool.

While the potato cools, grate the coconut and finely chop the cashew nuts and coriander.

Add these to the potato mixture., then squeeze in the juice of the lemon and lime.

Remove 2 sheets of filo and cut into 3 strips length-wise. These thinner strips will make delicate, pretty mouthfuls. Brush the filo with melted butter and place a teaspoon of the potato mixture near the top of the strip.

Roll the filling into the pastry, tucking in the sides as you go. Place on a baking sheet. Repeat as many times as necessary.

Finish by brushing the pastry tops with melted butter and sprinkle with black onion seeds/nigella.

Cook pastries in oven until crispy and golden.

*FILO *is so light and crisp, it's easily our favorite readymade pastry. The only thing to remember is to cover the pastry with a damp cloth when it's not being used. Filo dries out quickly and this will slow the process down.*

* *Look for* CREAMED COCONUT *in Middle Eastern specialty shops. Once you've tried this marvelous and versatile ingredient, you won't want to be without it.*

To stop creamed coconut from being too crumbly, put it in the freezer for 20 minutes before grating. Creamed coconut can be stored in the freezer for up to 12 months.

MUSHROOM, WHITE WINE, CREAM, BASIL AND SUN-DRIED TOMATO BRUSCHETTA

This hits the spot for a comfort-food starter. Or, serve
as a supper dish with a sharp salad and green beans.
Very easy and quick to make.

4 tablespoons olive oil

3 tablespoons / 25 grams butter

14 ounces / 400 grams chestnut mushrooms

1/2 cup / 125 milliliters white wine

handful basil, torn into bits

6 sun-dried tomatoes in oil

4 cloves garlic, thinly sliced

1/2 cup / 125 milliliters half and half / single cream

4 thin slices day-old baguette

Melt butter and 3 tablespoons olive oil together in a large saucepan over medium low.

Add garlic and cook until soft, but not colored.

Cut mushrooms into quarters. Turn up heat to medium and add to the garlic. Cook, stirring gently, for 5 minutes.

Pour on white wine, lower heat to medium-low and simmer until wine is reduced by half.

Remove from heat and add sun-dried tomatoes, cream and basil.

FOR THE BRUSCHETTA: Lightly brush the slices of baguette with olive oil and bake on a sheet in a preheated 400F / 200C oven until crisp and golden.

TO SERVE: Arrange the bruschetta on a plate and ladle the warm mushrooms on top.

sacred kitchen

All over the world, for as long as people have been cooking, the kitchen has been a place of great sacredness. Traditionally the heart of the home, it's where everyone meets at least once a day to share and replenish.

The kitchen is the place where storytelling happens, where household community assembles, where tears are shed and comfort is offered.

Many kitchens have shrines — small altars with a candle or picture of a sacred person. Zen Buddhists light a candle and bless the cooking space, the tools and food. In Hindi kitchens, offerings are made to Annapoorna, the goddess of nourishment. A ritual before cooking reminds us that we are more than the physical — that we are connected to each other and the divine when we prepare and eat food.

Light your own candle to remind yourself that you are part of nature, history and the great community of world cooks.

COURGETTE AND CORNMEAL FRITTERS WITH TZATZIKI DIP

A delicate starter which pleases the palate with its combination of soft and crunchy textures.

SERVES 2

3 medium zucchinis/courgettes

¼ cup / 50 grams fine cornmeal

pinch chili powder

2 eggs

4 tablespoons mild olive oil

1 cup / 250 grams Greek yogurt

1 teaspoon rock salt

½ cucumber (if possible Lebanese)*

2 cloves garlic

handful mint, finely chopped with a few leaves reserved for garnish*

*LEBANESE CUCUMBERS
are smaller and tend to be
less watery. They're also
sweeter and crunchier

*Substitute MINT
with lemon balm for
a mellower flavor.

FOR THE TZATZIKI: Cut the cucumber in half and remove the seeds with a teaspoon. Grate the halves and remove any liquid by placing in a clean tea towel and squeezing tightly.

Peel and crush garlic cloves with a teaspoon of rock salt.

Stir the crushed garlic and grated cucumber into the yogurt. Refrigerate until ready to serve.

Just before serving, add the chopped mint.

FOR THE ZUCCHINIS/COURGETTES: Wash, dry and cut zucchinis/courgettes into ½-inch / 1 centimeter slices.

Mix chili powder and cornmeal in a small bowl. In another bowl, beat the eggs.

In a large saucepan, heat oil over medium until a pinch of flour tossed in sizzles.

One by one, dip zucchini/courgette slices into cornmeal, shake, dip into beaten egg, then once more dip into cornmeal.

Fry gently in olive oil until golden.

TO SERVE: Arrange the fried zucchinis/courgettes on a plate and serve the tzatziki on the side with a garnish of mint or whichever herb you used.

FLATBREADS WITH SUMAC, THYME AND SESAME

These flatbreads are perfect as part of a tapas selection served with tabouli salad, creamy yogurt and flavored lemon oil. They're also a great snack by themselves, nibbled while drinking a glass of white wine after a heavy day at work.

Mix 2 teaspoons sumac, 1 teaspoon chopped fresh thyme and a teaspoon sesame seeds.

Brush a piece of flatbread or pita with olive oil and sprinkle with the herb and seed mix. Bake for a couple of minutes at 400F / 200C until golden.

SEED FLOURISHES

Mix a handful each of pumpkin, sesame and sunflower seeds on a baking tray. Stir in 1 tablespoon of soy sauce and bake at 350F / 180C for 10 minutes. Stir after 5 minutes. When cooled, the seeds will be crunchy. Eat as they are with a drink, or add to salads and savory stews for flavor and crunch.

PARMESAN WAFERS

Sophisticated *and* simple is such a seductive combination. In the culinary world, these delicate wafers are such best friends — their lacy good looks and crunchy-chewy deliciousness will never let you down.

Preheat oven to 350F / 180C.

Prepare a baking sheet covered with parchment paper.

Roughly grate 2 teaspoons Parmesan cheese and place in a mound on the parchment. Flatten the mound with the back of a teaspoon, sprinkle with black pepper and bake for a couple of minutes, or until golden.

Remove from the oven and drape over a rolling pin until cool — this will make a curved shape.

Repeat as many times as needed. Serve the wafers with risotto or by themselves as a nibble with drinks.

SHOPPING

FORAGING

What is shopping after all, but foraging. It is the hunting and unearthing of treasures and the ever-present possibility of surprise. This is especially true of markets where small producers bring their seasonal specialties. The displays of quality and freshness create natural oases in even the most urban of environments.

Taking the time to attune to food before it reaches the kitchen engenders a new attitude towards cooking and eating. Respect for the food and its origins is heightened, the delicate, complex web of connections between ourselves and the natural world makes itself seen. Likewise, in the smaller markets, the connections between grower, harvester, transporter, marketer and consumer become clearer.

SUPERMARKET ALCHEMIST

For an anthropologist — or a Martian — how riveting that in a society offering historically unprecedented plenty and choice, shopping for food has become a chore, a hassle, a source of stress.

I remember a group of teenagers brought over on a holiday from Romania to my local village soon after the overthrow of Ceausescu. Visiting the tiny village supermarket was so traumatic for them that plans for a trip to a city shopping center were hastily abandoned. The contrast between our overwhelming abundance and their paucity of choice on the shelves back home was extremely upsetting.

I marvel that having so much choice has become a challenge that can crush us to the point of paralysis. But for most of us, this bounty of supermarkets has created a blasé disconnection from the richness available to us and to the preciousness of these resources. Pleasure diminishes, radiance dims. I recently read that almost 80% of our shopping choices in supermarkets are semi-conscious. Easy to believe, as I myself can easily switch on auto-pilot to counteract the effects of fluorescent lights, the hum of fridges, the confusing layouts and crowds. In this way, food and its purchase become denuded of meaning and healthy choices are less likely to occur.

The times when I most enjoy shopping for food are often the times when I allow myself to appreciate what is being offered. Pleasure comes from taking the time to value shopping as an activity in its own right, not a means to another end. At such times I awaken to the significance of bounty and beauty in my life. These moments of appreciation arrive not when I'm struggling to get one task done so as to move onto the next, but when I'm fully present. Fully present, I view events as through a wide-angle lens and therefore am not easily knocked off center. There is a calmness and a steadiness in my actions, perhaps even joy. This is akin to the state

Buddhists call mindfulness. Mindfulness in daily life involves being aware of what we are doing as we are doing it, following our breath, watching the rise and fall of thoughts and emotions without a tight identification with them. We know that it is our interpretation of events that powers our reactions to them, not the events themselves.

As a child growing up in Denbigh, a small Welsh market town, going shopping was a great treat. At that time the town had ten or eleven "proper" grocery stores (now there are none). The one we frequented was called Owens and Davies. It was a long, cavernous shop with great mahogany counters and display cupboards down each side. When it came to our turn, the ritual began with a discussion of the family's health, the recommended choices of the day, and — best of all! — the unwrapping of a

huge slab of butter and the slicing of a piece for us to take home in greaseproof paper. Our food, the purchase of our food, held real significance for me.

I know! I know! It's different now, and very hard on a Friday evening when the supermarket is heaving, the kids are crying, the tills are down. But Phillippa and I talked to people who seemed to find both pleasure and nourishment in shopping for food. We asked them how they managed it. Their responses were illuminating. Why not see if any of these answers work for you?

- **Seeing the broader picture.** I cultivate a sense of huge appreciation and try to remember the connections we all have with one another. I'm connected to the girl at the till, the people who grew the food, the man who made the metal for the tractor, and hundreds more. We all depend on each other in this huge cooperative effort for me to get food on my plate.

- **Using visualization.** What best counteracts the sense of bombardment for me is imagining myself dancing up and down the aisles, plucking what I fancy here and there like fruit from a tree.

- **Finding the middle way.** I remember two visits to the same shop. One time I was in conflict between my desire for lots of good things and my guilt at spending too much money and eating meat, with endless calculations going round and round in my head. The next time I gave myself permission to buy a few things that were luxuries, but in small quantities; I felt really at peace.

- **Making it a treat.** I stock up on bulk buys of boring basics every month, then every few days leave work a little early to make a detour to a local specialist or a farm shop. This gives me fresh produce and new ideas to liven up what I already have.

- **Using it as a practice.** When the queues are especially long and I chose the wrong one, I try to remember my yoga practices and see it as an unwelcome but nevertheless valuable opportunity to practice calming breathing exercises and the attitude of total acceptance. I go home feeling really joyful and energized. —AB-J

main DISHES

In kitchen alchemy, liquid becomes cloud, bitter becomes sweet and an entire season dissolves on the tongue.

The tough becomes succulent and the hidden is revealed as a pinch of salt illuminates flavor.

The future becomes wholly present as beans soften and expand under the simple application of heat and water.

BAKED CAMEMBERT QUESADILLAS
WITH BLACK BEAN AND CHOCOLATE CHILI

SERVES 4

In the book *Like Water for Chocolate*, the heroine is born on a wooden kitchen table and spends her childhood lovingly learning how to cook. She is an emotional being, and her emotions always have an effect on the people who eat her food. One day she learns that the secret love of her life is going to marry her sister.

The setting is Mexico and it is hot. So hot that all the women need fans and the men heroically stand for long periods of time, swallowing the urge to faint. This is especially true at large events like weddings and funerals.

At her secret lover's wedding, our sad sister has to make all the food. And as she stirs and chops and kneads and cooks this particularly fine feast — after all, she wants only the best for her beloved — she can't help slip a little tear.

All the people are gathered. What a wonderfully happy occasion! Laughter fills the rooms. The old men and the women, the cousins and aunts, the bride and the groom, even the parrot smiles. They start to eat. But then the tear-stained food takes hold and one by one they start to cry. Soon the room is filled with deep weeping as the untold grief of the sad sister affects every single person. The rain starts, the storm gathers and the room grows dark until every person has cried out every grief he or she has ever known.

Then, because they cannot cry any more, they eat the chocolate cake and strangely feel much better, including the sad sister.

This recipe will not make you cry (unless of course you put in too much chili), but the chocolate has a good effect.

continued on page 90

BAKED CAMEMBERT QUESADILLAS
WITH BLACK BEAN AND CHOCOLATE CHILI (CONTINUED)

2 tablespoons olive oil

1 large white onion

2 carrots

2 zucchinis/courgettes

1 sweet potato

1 tablespoon cumin seeds

1 teaspoon ground cumin

2 teaspoons ground coriander

1/2 teaspoon salt

1 teaspoon chili powder

3 tablespoons tomato purée

1/4 cup / 50 grams sweet corn
(tinned or frozen)

1 15.5-ounce / 439-gram can
cooked black beans

2 ounces / 50 grams
very dark chocolate

3 ounces / 100-gram wedge
Camembert cheese

4 plain tortillas, corn or flour

bunch cilantro/fresh coriander,
chopped

FOR THE CHILI: Chop onion, carrots, zucchinis/courgettes and sweet potato into evenly-sized small chunks.

Sauté onion, carrots and sweet potato in the olive oil over medium-low heat until softened. Add cumin, coriander, salt and chili powder, cooking for a few minutes, occasionally stirring.

Add tomato purée and zucchinis/courgettes. Cover with water and bring to a boil, then simmer for 25 minutes.

Add sweet corn and black beans. Cook for a further 10 minutes. If the chili looks dry, add more water.

Break the chocolate into small pieces and add to the chili 15 minutes before serving so that it melts and mixes with the sauce — the chili should be off the heat. The chocolate gives the chili a wonderful depth of flavor.

FOR THE QUESADILLAS: Preheat oven to 350F / 170C.

Cut the Camembert into thin slices. Lay 2 tortillas on an ungreased baking tray and sprinkle with the cheese and cilantro/coriander. Top with the other 2 tortillas and bake in the oven until starting to crisp (just a few minutes). Cut into wedges and serve with the chili.

meditating with vegetables

Winter wonderland, freezing cold, the vegetables buried, hiding in the earth — they are hibernating, resting, snuggled deep.

Let's join them.

Find yourself a warm, private, cozy space. Sit in a comfortable chair. Take off your shoes and place your feet on the ground.

Rest your hands lightly in your lap, close your eyes and take a moment to listen to any noise outside your room. Can you hear the wind or rain beating against the window? Are the birds singing?

Start to notice sounds closer to you — is there a fire crackling, can you hear the clock ticking? Focus on the sounds within your own body and notice your breathing. Watch with your inner eye as your breath moves in and out of your body. Notice how your breath slows and you feel your body getting heavy and deeply relaxed.

Now imagine roots growing out of your toes, digging deep into the earth. Follow your roots down, down, and watch them curling and twisting, feeling at home in the earth of the mother Gaia. Your roots are red, the color of vibrancy, and they go deeper and deeper. Breathe and relax. Follow your roots as deep as they will go, through the layers of the earth, deeper and deeper until they come to the core. In the centre of the core is a small, radiant, glowing pool. Feel your roots resting in this pool; imagine this pool holds molten sunlight deep in the belly of Mother Earth. Breathe the golden light up through your roots, and into your body, nourishing, grounding and sustaining you.

Do this exercise whenever you feel in need of connection, grounding and relaxation.

THREE CHEESE, WILD GARLIC AND MINT PIE

This dish is delicious warm or cold. Eat with a nicely colored mixed green salad with good vinaigrette. Tzatziki served on the side is also a fine choice.

3 red onions

2 tablespoons olive oil

1 pound / 450 grams frozen spinach, defrosted or two large bags of fresh

1 package filo pastry (approx. 12 sheets)

2 tablespoons / 50 grams butter, melted

1 pound / 450 grams mixed cheeses: feta, cheddar, ricotta

3 big handfuls ramps/wild garlic*

2 eggs

3 big handfuls mint, chopped

3 tablespoons pine nuts/kernels, toasted

3 lemons

*If you can't get RAMPS/WILD GARLIC, add a bunch of chopped spring onions and 4 big cloves of garlic, peeled and finely sliced.

Preheat oven to 350F / 180C.

Peel and chop onion into a small dice. Sauté over medium-low heat in olive oil until translucent.

Add the spinach (if you're using frozen squeeze the water out first) and cook until tender.

In a large bowl, mix garlic, pine nuts and mint. Crumble in the feta, grate the cheddar, and stir in the ricotta.

Whisk the eggs and add along with squeezed lemon juice. Mix well.

Brush an 8-inch / 20-centimeter spring-release or loose bottom cake tin with melted butter. Top with one sheet of filo pastry. Brush the pastry with butter and top with more pastry. Continue in this way until you have used up half the packet. There should be an overlap of pastry and the sides should be covered. Now, spoon in the spinach/cheese mix. Layer 3 more buttered filo sheets on top, making sure to tuck into sides. Lastly, brush the remaining sheets with butter and scrunch up, placing them on top of the pie. Bake for about 25-30 minutes, or until crispy and golden.

TO SERVE: While still hot, remove from the pan and slice like a pie.

BARLEY RISOTTO

This is a dish that we like to cook in winter and early spring. Sometimes we add wild garlic at the end: the green of the leaves will melt into the barley and you can sprinkle the flowers on top along with a dollop of crême fraiche. Other variations can be made by adding lots of lemon juice and zest, or dill or chervil. Garnish these with slow-roasted cherry tomatoes and serve with skate wings or monkfish.

2 medium leeks, white part only

2 tablespoons / 30 grams butter

2 tablespoons olive oil

4 garlic cloves

sea salt

7 ounces / 200 grams chestnut mushrooms (about 12)

1 1/3 cups / 300 grams pearl barley

1 1/3 cups / 300 milliliters dry white wine

2 1/3 cups / 500 milliliters hot vegetable or chicken stock

1/2 cup / 125 milliliters heavy/double cream or crême fraiche

If you have any leftovers, make risotto cakes. Depending on the texture of your risotto, stir in a little beaten whole egg and sift in a little flour until the barley can be formed into a cake.

Shred finely the white of the leeks.

Heat the butter and oil over medium low until bubbling and add the leeks. Cook very gently without browning for about 10 minutes.

Crush the garlic cloves with a pinch of sea salt. Add to leeks and continue cooking for a few minutes — again without browning.

Slice mushrooms and add to the leek mixture.

Rinse barley. Raise heat to medium and add to the vegetables.

Stir in white wine, then add vegetable stock.

Bring the risotto to a very gentle simmer. It will take about 30 – 40 minutes to cook. Give an occasional stir, checking that the barley doesn't stick and add more liquid if needed. The cooked grain has a nutty, slightly chewy texture.

At the end of cooking and off the burner, stir in the cream or crême fraiche.

SWEET PEA SALSA WITH HOME BAKED CHIPS AND GRIDDLED TUNA

SERVES 4

This sauce could not be simpler nor deliver a brighter burst of flavor. We love that the intensity of its zingy freshness is perfectly matched by its sensational color. The sauce's creamy texture complements the tuna's dense chewiness and the salty grainy-ness of the chips.

FOR THE SALSA:

7 ounces / 200 grams frozen baby peas, cooked for 2 minutes

½ fresh jalapeño chili, very finely chopped

1 tablespoon sunflower oil

1 teaspoon ground cumin

1 teaspoon ground coriander

squeeze lime juice

pinch salt

Gently blend all ingredients to make a chunky sauce.

FOR THE CHIPS:

1 pound / 450 grams (2 – 3 large) King Edward potatoes, cut lengthwise into 1-inch / 2.5-centimeter fries or chips

3 – 4 tablespoons olive oil

Preheat oven to 400F / 200C.

Set a large pot of salted water to boil.

Plunge chips into boiling water for 2 minutes. Remove and drain, then blot on paper towel to remove remaining starch.

Place the chips on a baking tray and toss with oil until thoroughly coated.

Bake about 20 minutes, or until golden and crisp. Stir once during baking.

FOR THE TUNA:

4 fresh tuna steaks (one for each diner)

When the chips are half-cooked, start the tuna.

Lightly oil a large griddle or frypan with general cooking oil. Heat on medium. Cook steaks for 3 to 4 minutes on each side.

TO SERVE: Place a piece of tuna on each plate and spoon a little sauce on top. Pile the chips next to the tuna and eat with a green salad.

SUNSHINE FOOD

It's January cold: the sky is slate grey with edges of purple haze. Christmas is gone and the vegetables in our gardens have taken refuge underground — clearly a wise action. We're feeling in need of brightness and warmth. Into the kitchen then, to prepare some sunshine food.

From the garden take carrots

onions

leeks

turnips

parsnips and/or carrots

an orange pepper

rosemary

and garlic.

From the fridge, an orange pepper.

From the cupboard take chili oil

black cumin seeds

tomato purée

red lentils

vegetable stock

ketjap manis (an Indonesian sweet soy sauce)

creamed coconut

and tahini.

In a large soup pot, dry roast the black cumin seeds, stirring constantly over medium heat until they begin to release their wonderful, spicy aroma.

Add 2 teaspoons chili oil, and one handful each chopped onions, leeks, turnips, carrots, parsnips, orange pepper and 2 cloves garlic. Sauté for a few minutes.

Add 2 handfuls red lentils, 2 cups / 500 milliliters vegetable stock, 1 tablespoon tomato purée and half a sprig rosemary. Bring to a boil, then simmer very gently for an hour. Season with ketjap manis, and swirl in some tahini to taste. Add slivers of creamed coconut.

Be careful not to overcook – you don't want a mash, but a pool of creamy apricot liquid with chunks of golden vegetables. If you'd like, you can add more stock and make a soup, or noodles will make a laska (a spicy noodle dish). Or eat the stew with rice and sprinkle with nigella/black onion seeds for sharp and spicy contrast.

memories of food

It's 1990.

I'm in a flat in London, sitting on the floor with my Lebanese mother-in-law, making kibbeh, fasoulia and rich, pistachio-honeyed sweets while drinking tiny cups of very potent Arabic coffee. My mother-in-law speaks no English; I have only a smattering of Arabic — *yes, no* and *thank you*. My voluptuous sister-in-law, with her long black hair and laughing almond eyes, helps me squeeze minced lamb with cinnamon, allspice and bulgur wheat, then layer it with pine nuts and mint in a great silver-colored pan. Loud Arabic music transports us to a world of bright sunshine, veiled faces and the long wail of the mosque calling us to prayer. The heady scent of cardamom...

...and the sound of London traffic calling us back. —PL

BUTTERNUT WONTON RAVIOLIS

It was dark. The power was off — the freezer was getting warmer and the wonton
wrappers purchased for a special unspecified occasion were begging to be used.
I looked in my fridge (with a torch) for bean sprouts, chicken and Chinese herbs,
but instead found butternut squash, mascarpone cheese and Parmesan.
Well, who said Chinese and Italian aren't a good mix? —PL

SERVES 2

2 tablespoons / 25 grams red lentils

1 small butternut squash

2 tablespoons / 25 grams
mascarpone cheese

¼ cup / 50 grams grated Parmesan

good handful of fresh basil leaves,
shredded

2 tablespoons / 25 grams
breadcrumbs

2 tablespoons pine nuts/kernels

half lemon, squeezed

12 wonton wrappers

1 egg white

Preheat oven to 350F / 180C.

Cover lentils with water and cook until tender.

Slice squash in half, discard seeds and brush with olive oil. Bake, flesh
side down, until tender. When cooked, remove flesh and lightly mash.

Add mascarpone, Parmesan, basil leaves, breadcrumbs, pine nuts/
kernels, lemon juice and pepper to taste. Mix well.

To make the ravioli, place 1 teaspoon of the mixture in the middle of
a wonton wrapper. Brush the whisked egg white around the edge of
the wrapper, then lay another wrapper firmly on top. Press the edges
together with a fork. Repeat for all the wrappers.

In a large frypan, heat a little olive oil on medium. Place as many
raviolis as you can in the pan without crowding. Sauté until golden.
Add enough hot water to just cover the edges. Cover the pan. Steam
two minutes or until done. Remove and set aside in a warm place.
Pour out the water and repeat until all the raviolis are cooked.

TO SERVE: You may want to serve this with a tomato sauce, a creamy
lemon sauce, or simply melted butter with sage. The filling is also
great for roast peppers, eggplant/aubergines and zucchini/courgettes.

THAI-STYLE BUBBLE AND SQUEAK WITH SALMON FILLET

SERVES 4

Bubble and Squeak was the Monday dish in Britain in the 50s — it transformed the Sunday left-over vegetables and meat into a hearty favorite. This more exotic but equally easy version has developed its own following among our friends.

¾ pound / 300 grams (about 2 large or 3 medium) King Edward potatoes

1 bunch green / spring onions

half a red pepper

1 tablespoon sunflower oil

½ pound / 250 grams salmon fillet

¼ cup / 50 grams cilantro/coriander, finely chopped

2 tablespoons red Thai curry paste

2 tablespoons / 25 grams grated creamed coconut

4 tablespoons frozen peas, defrosted

Peel potatoes and chop into regular-sized pieces. Boil in salted water until cooked. Drain and set aside to cool.

Clean and chop spring onions finely. Wash red pepper and cut into small, even pieces.

In a frying pan, heat the sunflower oil over medium-low, then add onions and pepper. Cook gently until the vegetables are soft and slightly colored.

Roughly mash the cooked potatoes and add to the frying pan. Continue cooking on medium heat, stirring every now and again until the potatoes crisp.

Cut the salmon into 1-inch pieces. Add to the frying pan and cook for 4 minutes. Stir in the red Thai paste, grated coconut, cilantro/coriander and peas. Continue cooking until the salmon is done — just a couple of minutes or less.

TO SERVE: The Bubble and Squeak can be eaten like this, perhaps with steamed broccoli. Make a more elegant meal by shaping the mix into cakes, dipping them in flour and frying in olive oil on each side until golden. Serve with **Creamy Coconut and Coriander Sauce,** page 117.

HOT BUTTERED SMOKED SALMON
WITH GINGERED SWEET POTATO MASH

SERVES 2

This dish is a treat. The smoked salmon becomes wonderfully robust when cooked in this way — it almost tastes like bacon! We like to serve it with something plain and green, like steamed broccoli, to counteract the richness.

1 pound / 500 grams (2–3 large) sweet potatoes, peeled and cut into regular chunks

1 tablespoon olive oil

1 red onion, thinly sliced

1-inch piece ginger, peeled and grated

1 teaspoon cumin seeds

2 tablespoons / 30 grams unsalted butter

½ pound / 200 grams smoked salmon, sliced into 1-inch strips

1 lemon

Boil sweet potato in salted water until soft. Drain and mash.

Heat the olive oil in a frying pan over medium-low. Add onion, ginger and cumin seeds, cooking gently until soft.

Stir the onion mixture into the sweet potato mash and put aside, keeping it warm.

In the same frying pan, add the butter and heat over medium. Sauté the salmon in the butter for a minute or two, or until it starts to curl and color.

Serve this on a platter. Spoon the salmon over the mash and top with any juices. Finish with a generous squeeze of lemon.

POLENTA CAKES WITH CHESTNUT, FENNEL, MUSHROOM, RED WINE AND PROVENÇAL HERB RAGOUT

SERVES 6

Imagine golden, crusty, cheesy polenta cakes covered with a rich Burgundy ragout sprinkled with fresh green parsley. This is comfort at its most comforting. The polenta pops and sputters and sometimes likes to jump out of the pan. Be careful of your arms and show it who's in charge!

FOR THE POLENTA CAKES
(can be made a day ahead)

2 cups / 500 milliliters water

1 stick / 50 grams butter

$^1/_2$ cup / 125 grams polenta

2 egg yolks

$^1/_4$ cup / 50 grams grated cheddar, plus more for sprinkling

handful fresh thyme, chopped

Preheat oven to 350F / 180C.

Heat the water to simmer. Add the polenta in a slow continuous stream, stirring constantly — a whisk is good for this. Simmer gently for about 10 minutes. When the polenta's done, it gets thick and comes away from the edge of the pan when stirred.

Add the butter, whisked egg yolks, cheese and thyme. Season to taste.

Pour the polenta onto a greased baking tin and spread evenly. Allow to cool.

20 minutes before serving, sprinkle with some extra cheese, cut into wedges and place in the oven. Bake until golden.

continued on page 104

POLENTA CAKES WITH CHESTNUT, FENNEL, MUSHROOM, RED WINE AND PROVENÇAL HERB RAGOUT (CONTINUED)

FOR THE RAGOUT

4 ounces / 125 grams dried
porcini mushrooms

3 red onions

2 bulbs fennel

4 sticks celery

4 carrots

8 ounces / 250 grams chestnut
mushrooms

4 garlic cloves

4 tablespoons olive oil

1¼ cups / 300 milliliters dry red wine

1½ cups / 350 milliliters vegetable stock

1 tablespoon tomato purée

4 ounces / 125 grams tinned unsweetened
chestnut purée

handful fresh mixed herbs (rosemary,
thyme, oregano)

handful flat leaf parsley

1 red pepper

4 ounces / 125 grams chestnuts

4 ounces / 125 grams sun-dried tomatoes

Preheat oven to 350F / 170C.

Soak the dried porcini mushrooms in ½ cup / 100 milliliters hot water.

Peel and cut red onions into quarters. Remove the woody bits from the fennel and cut into quarters. Cut celery into chunks. Peel and cut carrots into small chunks. Slice the mushrooms in half. Crush the garlic with a little salt.

Lightly sauté the carrots, fennel, red onions, red pepper and celery until just softened. Arrange them in a large baking dish.

In the same pan, sauté the chestnut mushrooms and garlic for a couple of minutes on low heat. Turn up the heat to medium and add the wine, stock, tomato purée, chestnut purée, porcini mushrooms, sun-dried tomatoes and chestnuts. Cook until lightly colored.

Pour this liquid mix over the vegetables in baking dish.

Sprinkle on the mixed fresh herbs and season with salt and pepper.

Cover the dish with foil and bake for 45 minutes. Check occasionally and add water if dry. After removing from the oven, sprinkle with fresh parsley.

TO SERVE: Arrange a large slice of polenta on a plate and half cover with ragout. Garnish with a sprig of parsley or fennel.

LEMON ROAST CHICKEN

This is a simple feast. Tender chicken juices mix with the roasting vegetables and the lemon becomes golden-burnt at the edges, tasting sour and sweet.

SERVES 2 PEOPLE FOR ONE MEAL AND
1 PERSON FOR NEXT DAY PICKING

1 small free range chicken, approximately 2.6 pounds / 1.2 kilos

2 lemons

3 medium carrots, cut into long strips

2 big parsnips, cut into long strips

3 medium roasting potatoes, cut into small, even chunks

3 tablespoons olive oil

4 tablespoons / 50 grams butter

sea salt

sprig fresh rosemary

5 large cloves garlic

tin foil to cover chicken

Preheat oven to 400F / 200C.

Place washed and dried chicken in deep roasting tray.

Cut 1 lemon in quarters and place inside chicken.

Arrange carrots, parsnips and potatoes around the chicken.

Cut the other lemon into wedges and add to vegetables.

Dribble olive oil over vegetables and chicken. Mix well.

Put knobs of butter over chicken skin.

Chop rosemary and sprinkle over vegetables and chicken.

Season with sea salt and place in the oven.

Every 10 – 15 minutes, turn vegetables so they brown evenly.

About halfway into the cooking, add the whole cloves of garlic with skin still on to the roasting vegetables and lightly top the chicken with tin foil to keep it from burning. Cook for 1 hour or until juices run clear.

After cooking, let the chicken rest for 5 minutes before carving.

TO SERVE: Serve this on a large platter. It's a treat to unwrap the garlic and squeeze over the roasted vegetables and lemon on your plate. The chicken is wonderful served with a zingy rocket, spinach and chard salad.

RHYTHM

REDISCOVERING THE ART OF SLOWNESS

I recently had the pleasure of cooking for a group of friends in the wilds of Scotland on a retreat holiday. The house was set on an isolated peninsula in the northwest. There were no roads and only two ways to get there — by boat or by foot, three and a half miles around a mountain! We didn't have a boat so we loaded everything we needed for the week into our rucksacks and set off, single file, on the rocky, gorse-hedged mountain track. The fine Scottish rain started to fall, and our bodies felt weighted with the heaviness of our packs. But as we neared our destination, I realized that a change had occurred: I had become aware of nature around me. The sun appeared and the rocks sparkled crystalline in the bright light. I could hear the sea lapping in the distance, a tiny frog leapt from a puddle into thick grass and a coconut scent wafted from the gorse. I had started to engage my senses and feel connected to my surroundings.

The house manifested itself as a large granite square dotted with small windows. It looked like a stronghold secure enough to fight pirates, wild beasts and the inclement weather.

In the kitchen, there was a range that had to be lit each day, a huge wooden table and enough space to cook and talk to friends at the same time. As there was only a tiny windmill for electricity, appliances like a food processor, electric grinder, whisk, breadmaker, and even music were absent. (What would I do without the food processor? And have you noticed how many recipes cannot work without them?) But no matter: I had decided that in my busy life, this week would be about healing and the art of slowness.

Each day I lit a candle and imagined the kitchen as a healing sanctuary. I invoked that everything I cooked would be a gift and would radiate the energy of joy. I attempted to be truly present while cooking; I would pay attention to the textures, rhythms and sounds of what I did. The lack of electrical helpmates became a doorway into a rich

BLESS THIS

Most spiritual traditions advocate blessing our food, as both thanksgiving and offering. We believe blessings change the subtle energies available to us from food, but it also changes us — slows us down, attunes us, helps us be more receptive to these energies. This practice can be as simple as pausing for a few moments and imagining love flowing from our hearts through our hands and into the food in front of us.

experience of connection to the ingredients and the art. Peace permeated me as I became one with the beating of eggs into butter, the fine sifting of flour falling lightly into the bowl and the slurping of liquids being incorporated round and round into the carrot cake.

Now, for a trained cook to deliberately slow her movements is not easy. I can chop cucumbers for the Olympics, whisk meringues into snow drifts and throw together a fabulous chocolate cake while stirring ten sauces and making the salad for lunch! And I admit there were meals on this holiday when I didn't always manage "slowness" or "peace." I did learn, however, to re-engage my senses, all of them — sight, sound, taste, smell, touch and that extra sense of intuition. I also learned to take a break between cooking and eating. I cooked as much as I wanted in the morning, went for a long wild walk in the afternoon, watched seals and didn't swim in the icy sea. When I returned I was refreshed and could finish the cooking in a relaxed and renewed way.

Returning to my busy life, I have consciously used my experience of slowness as a lodestone for transformation. When finding myself stressed, with lots to do and not enough time, I stop for a moment. I listen to my breathing as it moves in and out of my body. I smell the aroma in the kitchen, I sense the weight of my clothes on my body and I look at my ingredients. I think about the meal I am preparing and the people I am cooking for; I visualize happy faces eating radiant food. Magically, time stretches and I am able to do everything with ease. Try it and see. —PL

THE CHOCOLATE MEDITATION

Quite possibly, chocolate is not the first thing that comes to mind when you think of meditation.

However, meditation is defined as the process of effortlessly directing our attention in a sustained way onto an object, be it something external, such as the flame of a candle or a sacred symbol, or an inner object such as a mantra, or the breath, or — the taste of chocolate!

In business workshops, I often give people a calming break with the Chocolate Meditation. Fine chocolate of intense flavor is brought in on a beautiful platter and everyone is offered a piece. We hold it for a moment, taking in its appearance, its smell, its weight in our hands. Then we eat it in silence, as slowly as we are able, being as present as possible to its taste and texture in our mouths. It can take five minutes to eat one small square!

People sometimes find this a revelation of taste, of appreciation, of slowing down time. To slowly eat can calm, allowing us to catch up with ourselves and create space between our center and whatever is preoccupying us. In this way, that one piece can be perfectly satisfying all by itself.

Next time you reach for the chocolate on auto-pilot, really stop and give yourself chocolate. Take time out from whatever it is you're doing. If you're at home, switch off the television. If you're at your desk, walk to your nearest point of fresh air. If you're driving, stop in a lay-by. Spend five whole delicious minutes absorbing yourself in the simple act of eating your chocolate. —AB-J

vitaLity sauces

MAHANIRVANA TANTRA

May the ocean of "self"

The ocean of honey,

The ocean of wine,

The ocean of ghee,

The ocean of curd,

The ocean of sweet water,

Sprinkle thee with these consecrated waters.

AVOCADO, LIME, CORIANDER AND PUMPKIN OIL SAUCE

A rich green sauce flecked with fresh coriander.

2 ripe avocados

1 lime

handful cilantro/fresh coriander, roughly chopped

¾ cup / 175 milliliters pumpkin oil

sea salt

Cut the avocados in half and remove the stones. Scoop the flesh into the bowl of a blender. Squeeze in lime and add the coriander and oil. Mix on medium speed. If the sauce is too thick, add a dash of hot water. Season to taste.

TO SERVE: Serve drizzled over any white fish, or creamy cheese with rye bread, or fresh tomatoes and rock salt, or pasta.

CREAMY COCONUT AND CORIANDER SAUCE

This light sauce with a hint of lemon blends wonderfully with
the **Thai-style Bubble and Squeak** (page 100).

1 14-ounce tin coconut milk

bunch cilantro/fresh coriander, chopped

1 stalk lemongrass

Split the lemongrass open from its stem and lightly hit with a rolling pin.

In a medium-sized pan, heat the coconut milk slowly with the
lemongrass until warm. Turn off the heat and allow to infuse for an hour.

Discard lemon grass and blend the liquid in a processor with the
coriander.

If you would like to make the sauce a bit thicker, add $\frac{1}{2}$ cup grated
creamed coconut and heat gently, stirring until thickened.

TO SERVE: Serve this hot with chicken and fish dishes.

LITTLE BLACK DRESS SAUCE

This is a basic of the sauce world. It can be used as-is with pasta or dressed up with mint and raisins/sultanas to give a dish a Moroccan flavor. Crème fraiche will tone it down for fish. Add rosemary at the beginning of cooking to team with lamb.

This sauce is perfect served with polenta, roasted Mediterranean vegetables and Haloumi cheese. It can also be reduced until very thick, then frozen in ice cube trays for a last moment addition to wintry lentil soups.

2 red onions

2 tablespoons olive oil

3 garlic cloves

2 2/3 cups / 400 grams chopped tomatoes (tinned is good)

2 ounces / 50 grams tinned anchovies in oil

1/2 cup / 125 milliliters dry red wine

1 1/4 cups / 300 milliliters water

pinch of sugar

Slice onion finely and cook slowly over medium-low heat in the olive oil for 10 minutes.

Crush garlic with a little salt and add to the onions. Cook for a further 3 minutes.

Add wine, tomatoes, anchovies, sugar and water. Cook for about 30 minutes on a very low simmer. You'll know it's cooked when the anchovies fall apart and disappear into the sauce. Your sauce will be rich, deep red and glossy. If too thick, you can always add more water.

AIOLI

Last year in northern Spain, a group of us embarked on a cooking retreat. The sun was bright and the markets were stunning. Vegetables were piled high in rainbow colors. The fish just fresh from the sea — blues, greens and silvery mirrored mackerel lay alongside heaps of tiny glinting fish for frying. We had the choice of numerous olives, nuts, capers, jars of handmade tomato chutneys and big green bunches of local herbs.

Aioli works outstandingly with most Mediterranean dishes. We returned to our villa kitchen to make salt-baked bream with Lyonnaise potatoes and a wild herb salad. The slow cooked garlic in this recipe gives a sweeter, less pungent finish — nice with baked or steamed fish, steamed or roasted vegetables. —PL

6–8 garlic cloves

1 teaspoon Dijon mustard

pinch sugar

2 egg yolks

1 cup / 250 milliliters olive oil

2 tablespoons lemon juice

seasoning

Preheat oven to 350F / 180C.

Place the garlic cloves on a baking sheet with the skins on and roast until soft; about 20 minutes.

Pop the garlic from their skins and place in a blender with the mustard, sugar and egg yolks. Turn the blender on low, and add the oil very, very slowly.

Finish with lemon juice and seasoning to taste. If too thick, add a tablespoon hot water.

CREAMY GREEN GODDESS, BASIL AND TOFU SAUCE

Pour over grain and legume salads. It also works as a coleslaw dressing, and is marvelous with fish and fried tofu salads served with rice on the side.

standard 8-ounce / 220-gram package plain tofu

1 bunch basil

²/₃ cup / 150 milliliters crème fraiche

1 teaspoon tahini

Put all the ingredients in food processor and blend.
To make it even more creamy, add mayonnaise to taste.

JALAPEÑO TAPENADE

SERVES 6

There used to be a wonderful vegetarian restaurant called the Red
Herring, a delightful oasis in what was quite a run down part of
Newcastle. Here was where I first tasted this fabulous tapenade with
homemade bread and a salad of wild leaves and flowers. While tapenade
is certainly a starter, we've included it here because it also makes a
delicious addition to soups and pasta sauces. —PL

2 cups / 500 grams kalamata olives, stoned

1 or 2 jalapeños / chilies, deveined and seeded

4 garlic cloves

4 tablespoons red vinegar

½ cup / 120 milliliters olive oil

1 cup / 250 grams ground almonds

1 bunch fresh basil

Finely chop the chilies.

Crush the garlic cloves.

Put all the ingredients in a food processor and blend to a
smooth texture. Add more almonds if the mix is too wet.

Serve with good bread or add to pasta and soups. The tapenade
will keep for up to a week in the fridge.

FLOURISHES:
FRESH GREEN BUTTER

Flavored butters are a perfect, quick way to add flavor, texture and color to pasta, steaks, fish and vegetables. Probably the most famous flavored butter is garlic — added to bread, heated in the oven and served crispy, with a melting middle dripping with garlic and herbs.

    The French use a mix of butter and flour to thicken and add a glossy finish to stews and sauces; you can add your own flavored butter for the same effect.

Flavored butters can be kept up to a year in your freezer. Keep a stock handy and the next time you cook a steak, add a ¼-inch slice while the steak is still hot — watch the butter turn into instant sauce.

TO MAKE A BASIC GREEN HERB FLAVORED BUTTER:

Chop 2 large handfuls of green herbs (flat leaf parsley, thyme, basil, lemon balm).

In a mixing bowl, stir the herbs into 2 sticks / 8 ounces softened unsalted butter.

Cut a rectangle of waxed paper, 12 inches by 6 inches. Using your hands, mold the butter into a rough roll in the middle of the rectangle. Roll up the waxed paper and twist both ends — the end result will look something like a sausage shape. Chill in the fridge or freezer (at least half hour in fridge), slice into ¼-inch rounds when needed.

OTHER IDEAS FOR FLAVORED BUTTERS:

Lemon zest, dill and anchovy
Pesto and basil
Sun-dried tomato and olive
Tarragon
Blue cheese and mustard
Chili, cilantro / coriander and lime zest

LEMON INFUSED OIL

Oils make a wonderful carrier for herbs, chilis and whole spices and are very easy to make. Gently heating the oil will encourage the flavors to seep into the oil.

Heat about 2 cups / 500 milliliters extra virgin olive oil and the zest of two lemons gently in a pan until just warm. Decant into a clear glass bottle. Keep in fridge and use within 2 months.

Lemon Infused Oil makes a lovely subtle salad dressing mixed with mild mustard and sweet slow-cooked garlic cloves. It can be dribbled as it is over fish, pasta, lamb and grilled vegetables and adds an extra dimension to soups, stews and mashed potatoes.

When using herbs, try the woody ones such as thyme, rosemary and bay. Make sure the herbs and whole spices are dry before adding to the oil.

HeaLing

THE GUILT ON THE GINGERBREAD

Assured abundance of high-quality food is something we in the West take for granted. This paradise of food is reflected in the wealth of cookbooks, magazine articles and television programs celebrating the almost limitless possibilities. At the same time there is also a parallel and powerful flood of media attention on food as danger, as a threat, as the enemy.

As a society, we are deeply conflicted about what we eat. In the UK, the world's sixth richest economy, sales of organic food and healthy-eating books grow rapidly, yet four million people are clinically malnourished. Our takeaways, school meals and convenience foods are amongst the unhealthiest in the world, being largely composed of poor-quality ingredients skillfully synthesized to seduce. Celebrity ideals of desirability grow smaller as we ourselves grow larger.

As individuals, many of us worry about the safety of our food. We obsess about what we should and shouldn't eat to be slim, to be healthy, to be conscious; we arrange our lives around endless calculations of calorie and nutrient content. As we seek to control our appetite for food, often as a subconscious means of proving to ourselves and others by our slenderness that we are together enough to at least control something in our lives, private rituals around eating are becoming common. Food exclusions are also burgeoning, with cooking dinner for guests becoming a minefield as one may be wheat-intolerant, another avoiding dairy (except for sheeps' milk products, don't forget!), another not eating the minutest amount of sugar or salt.

Our innocence around food has gone. Eating is loaded — a simple bodily pleasure has become a series of complex cerebral problems and daily navigations. Fear and guilt predominate. A lack of trust in nutritional information, our own bodies, and our ability to make choices leaves us tense, uncertain, and above all, disconnected. One-sixth of our food budget goes toward packaging, and one-third of the food we buy becomes landfill because we consistently purchase more than we can eat or are prepared to cook.

How did this happen?

Interest in the quality of our food is healthy and necessary, but somehow this useful instinct has ballooned out of balance, perhaps because the origins and the processing of food is now so hard to see due to the myriad stages between field and plate. There has been so much change in food growing, processing and marketing, and so much media scrutiny on those changes that keeping abreast can easily become overwhelming. Statistics of glycaemic indices, ecological footprints, vitamin levels, omega-oil proportions, fair trade credentials and sugar levels all swirl around in our heads as we search for a fast and simple lunch.

Let's move towards a personal truce amidst the paradoxes by accepting that the complexities exist, but so does the simple joy of food and eating. We can help to heal the schisms between mind and body, where the inner statistician orchestrates our natural appetites, through relearning by focusing on those foods we are drawn to and which bring us real well-being, and therefore healthy satisfaction.

THE DISH

Many years ago, I wandered through the just-becoming-fashionable Marais quarter of Paris. Back then, it was a beguiling mixture of the neglected and the fantastical; rundown buildings studded with the occasional gem of a designer shop or an artist's studio with its witty, magpie offerings.

Even so, I was exhausted. Paris was overwhelming me.

Then I came upon the most magical teahouse. Its old woodwork was painted plum and dark green, and murals of Alice in Wonderland characters appeared on the sandy walls inside. I sank gratefully into one of the faded armchairs, a motley assortment of which surrounded each wonky wooden table.

I was the only customer, and the quietness was infinitely healing. It was so comfortable, I meditated and actually fell asleep after eating the most delicious homemade ice cream. Scoops were piled high on a glass cake-stand — coconut, mango, rich vanilla, pistachio, coffee. Crisp homemade lacy biscuits and an embossed doily perfected the dish — I was in heaven!

Beautiful china and glass transform what we eat; the right unmatching teacup and saucer can turn a snack into a ceremony. For example, just imagine if they had served the ice cream in an orange plastic bowl! How about your fragrant first cup of morning coffee swirling in a chipped mug advertising widgets? The homemade liqueur truffles presented to you by your friend in a neon cardboard pizza box?

Experiment with this minimal feng shui of form and beauty. Serve lunchtime tomato soup in the family heirlooms. Scour junk shops for treasure. Play with contrasts and harmonies between the food you eat and what you put it in — today try beetroot in a gold dish, tomorrow in earthy peasant pottery. Ask yourself how that affects the flavor and the experience. Aim to totally delight yourself with this secret daily pleasure. —AB-J

sweets

The two core meanings of the word *sweet* are inextricably woven together, signifying that which is *beloved* and *delightful* to the *sense* and the *heart*. As one of the fundamental tastes of nature, sweetness represents a purity, a distillation of the essence of pleasure.

Sweetnesses of all kinds have had a role in enhancing our lives, for even the tiniest portions can ripple out into waves of well-being. In the British Isles, this might translate into the hallowed ritual of stopping whatever you are doing at four o'clock and sitting down with tea, friends and fabulous cakes. It could mean morning elevenses (exactly the same except that coffee replaces tea) or a surprise mid-week dessert to lift the spirits. The cookery writer Nigel Slater goes so far as to call puddings "medicine" because of their healing and comforting effects. Experiment with the following dishes and start a new tradition with your friends!

PEAR, PISTACHIO, CHOCOLATE AND CARDAMOM CAKE

MAKES 1 SMALL LOAF

This is an easy-peasy and fail-safe cake which could easily become your posh signature offering for all cake-worthy occasions. It's perfect straight out of the oven with the chocolate still melting and served with yogurt or cream. While the combination of cardamom, chocolate and pear is sublime, the addition of crunchy, pale-green pistachio nuttiness makes this cake heaven!

1¼ cups / 150 grams all purpose/plain flour

1 teaspoon baking powder

¾ cup / 150 grams superfine/caster sugar

¾ cup / 150 grams unsalted butter

3 eggs

7 ounces / 200 grams chocolate (Green and Black's dark orange is good)

12 cardamom pods

¾ cup / 200 grams pistachio nuts

1 teaspoon vanilla

2 pears

Preheat oven to 350F / 180C and grease a small loaf tin.

Place flour, baking powder, sugar, butter and eggs in a food processor. Blend until just combined (about 1 minute). Transfer to a mixing bowl.

Break chocolate into small squares.

Split cardamom pods, take out seeds and roughly crush.

Chop the pistachios coarsely.

Peel, core and chop pear into rough, ¼-inch pieces.

Add chocolate, cardamom, pistachios, vanilla and pear to the cake mix. Pour into loaf tin and bake in the oven for about 45 minutes or until skewer comes out clean.

ORANGE AND ALMOND DESSERT

SERVES 8

This cake is inspired by Claudia Roden, one of our favorite cookery writers. We've used less sugar and added candied orange peel to give some texture. Wheat- and fat-free, this cake can double as a dessert / pudding served with Greek yogurt. For an extra kick, you can add Cointreau at the end of baking.

2 oranges

6 eggs

2 tablespoons orange blossom water

3/4 cup / 200 grams light brown sugar

1 teaspoon baking powder

2 cups / 250 grams ground almonds

1 tablespoon / 30 grams crystallized orange peel, chopped

5 tablespoons Cointreau (optional)

Wash the oranges and boil them whole for 2 hours, or until very soft.

Beat the eggs with the sugar.

Add orange blossom water, baking powder, almonds and candied peel.

Purée the whole oranges in a food processor and stir into the almond mix.

Preheat oven to 300F / 150C.

Grease and line an 8-inch / 23-centimeter cake tin. Add the cake mix and bake for about an hour, or until firm.

Out of the oven and while still warm, make 4 or 5 holes in the cake with cocktail sticks and dribble in the Cointreau.

Another bonus is that the liquid from boiling the oranges can be used as a face tonic before moisturizing. Keep it in the fridge and it will last for a few days.

starLight souffLé

What happens when we make a soufflé?

We whip the egg whites and beautiful peaks of dry white clouds appear. Carefully folding them into the sauce, we put the dish into the oven with a prayer — or at least a lot of hope, as there is always an unpredictable element.

Twenty minutes later, we open the oven and with luck, an impossibly glorious dish emerges and is proudly carried to table.

A soufflé's firm but fragile exterior conceals the inner creaminess. It must be eaten immediately or the magic will deflate, and this transitoriness is in itself part of the mystique.

So — what really happens when we make a soufflé?

Heavy becomes light, liquid becomes solid. The ordinary is transformed into delight and surprise. In this way the soufflé is the perfect symbol for the way food can be transformed, and in doing so it is *we* who are transformed.

coffee and chocolate

I often wonder why certain ingredients such as chocolate and coffee play such a special role in so many lives around the world. Yes, of course I have read the scientific explanations about the minerals they provide, the caffeine high, and at a more subconscious level, chocolate's sensual stimulation due to its melting-point being so fortuitously close to blood heat. But I've always felt that there's a large element of mystery in the spell they cast.

I vividly remember a newspaper article by Germaine Greer over a decade ago describing her visit to the very basic one-room hut occupied by an Ethiopian family living at the very margins of existence. Through all their difficulties they had somehow managed to give themselves one cup of coffee each day. This has great significance in Ethiopian culture, original home of coffee. As her host breathed a few twigs into a fire and roasted some green beans in a small and very battered pan, Greer's expectations were not high. To her tremendous surprise, the coffee was the best of her life — earthy, winey, searingly intense.

This to me is a powerful and poignant story – a considerable proportion of their meager income was spent on coffee; it provided no calories but greatly nourished the spirit. The food and drink we ingest make up the cells of our bodies, but their cultural significance is no less profound. It's one of the strongest ways in which we make ourselves who we are. We reinforce our identity and community through shared rituals of eating and drinking.

Potency of flavor can stop us in our tracks, warm us up to life, startle us into the present moment. The Incas discovered how to make chocolate drinks, spiced with chili, and prized it highly for its mystical significance; monks of old in their midnight cells nursed pots of coffee to maintain their vigils of prayer; early-morning espressos propel modern Italians into their day. Certain foods and drinks link us across time and space as they metamorphose into new forms which continue to hold their power over us. —AB-J

RICH CHOCOLATE SOUFFLÉS WITH MELTING MARMALADE MIDDLES

These soufflés take chocolate and (almost unbearably!) intensify its blissful melting quality, the coffee contributes a dark depth to the flavor, and the marmalade middles bring the eater a surprise *wow*.

1 tablespoon / 25 grams soft butter

¼ cup / 60 milliliters single cream/half and half

3½ ounces / 100 grams dark chocolate, broken into small pieces

1 teaspoon instant coffee granules

2 eggs, separated

¼ cup / 50 grams superfine/caster sugar

4 teaspoons chunky orange marmalade

créme fraiche or cream

Preheat oven to 400F / 200C.

Grease 4 ramekins with butter and set aside.

In a heat-proof bowl, place cream, chocolate and coffee granules. Set the bowl over a pan of simmering water until the ingredients have melted. Allow to cool slightly.

In another bowl, beat egg whites until they form stiff peaks. Gradually whisk in the sugar.

Mix the egg yolks into the chocolate. Lightly fold the chocolate mixture into the egg whites.

Fill each of the ramekins halfway with the soufflé. Spoon 1 teaspoon marmalade into each dish, then finish filling with the remaining soufflé.

Bake in the oven for about 10 minutes. Serve warm with a dollop of créme fraiche or cream.

CHOCOLATE AND COCONUT TART

This wonderfully rich, melt-in-your mouth crust and intensely chocolate dessert is a really decadent finish to any dinner party. It's also both dairy- and gluten-free. Thank you Paula Young at the Lancrigg Hotel and vegetarian restaurant for allowing us to use this recipe.

FOR THE CRUST

1/3 cup / 80 grams cashews

1/2 cup / 125 grams rice flour

1/3 cup / 75 grams raw cane sugar

pinch of salt

3 1/2 ounces / 100 grams dairy-free margarine

Preheat oven to 325F / 170C.

Blend cashews in a food processor until finely chopped. Mix in the rice flour, salt and sugar.

Melt the margarine and stir into the dry ingredients.

Press into a 9-inch / 23-centimeter flan tin and bake for 20 minutes.

Allow to cool.

FOR THE FILLING

14 ounces / 400 grams dark chocolate

2 1/2 cups / 600 milliliters coconut milk

Gently melt the chocolate with the coconut milk in a heavy-bottomed pan. Stir continuously until well mixed. Pour over the crust and allow to cool. Refrigerate.

TO SERVE: Cut into wedges. This cake is utterly delicious served with cream.

For a quick alternative crust, mix 1 cup / 200 grams graham crackers or digestive biscuits and 1 tablespoon butter in a food processor. Press into the tin.

BLUEBERRY ROSE FIGS: AN AUGUST RECIPE

Acquire some beautiful black figs.

Lay them outdoors in a dish to absorb some warmth.

Find a few handfuls of blueberries.

Perhaps you will pick up a precious box in a supermarket, or maybe you'll forage in your favorite woods or moors for each tantalizingly hidden berry.

Put the berries in a pan and cover with water, a little sugar, and the petals from the most fragrant rose you can find.

Put the lid on the pan and simmer with the greatest delicacy. Cool and strain the syrup into a jug.

Bring out the figs. Place one per person on large and attractive plates. Decorate with dark pink hollyhock petals and drizzle on the blueberry-rose syrup.

Cremé fraiche is a delicious possibility, but in no way essential.

august

The opposing
of peach and sugar,
and the sun inside the afternoon
like the stone in the fruit.

The ear of corn keeps
its laughter intact, yellow and firm.

August,
the little boys eat
brown bread and delicious moon.

— FEDERICO GARCÍA LORCA

ORCHIDS for breakfast

The single biggest improvement in the quality of my life over the past few years has come from changing the way I eat breakfast.

Picture me in the past, kneeling on the floor in front of a tall mirror, simultaneously shoveling down mouthfuls of cereal, getting dressed, applying make-up and sorting the day's work papers. I would frequently jump up for something I had forgotten, or to sort out the washing, before rushing out the door.

The exhaustion of my morning rhythm led to a fresh way of organizing my time. I now eat breakfast in the company of my orchids. I sit at my dining room table, and if it's dark I light a candle. I look out at the birds and bushes and sky. I notice microscopic changes in any new orchid shoots or buds since the previous evening and am nourished by their symbolism of endless possibilities emerging seemingly from nowhere.

And I eat muesli made sublime by the addition of red grapes, raspberries, blueberries and a most generous dousing of Green and Black's sexy dark cocoa powder. With this I drink freshly-ground coffee with cream floating on top.

The intense flavors (and of course the caffeine) wake me up to the present, to this morning now. I may only sit there for fifteen minutes, but the difference to my day has been profound. I feel connected with the day's priorities, more in control and peacefully in balance. —AB-J

THE HUMMINGBIRD DIPS ITS TONGUE IN LIQUID HAPPINESS

(With thanks to the poet Mary Oliver for the title, inspired by a poem of breath-catching beauty entitled "The Hummingbird Pauses at the Trumpet Vine.")

This dish consists of several small ramekins on a big platter, each filled with flavored hot chocolate of rich and creamy consistency. Into the pots dip all sorts of delicious fingers of food, rather like sweet versions of the buttered soldiers we eat with soft-boiled eggs.

INGREDIENTS FOR THE HOT CHOCOLATE

1 cup / ½ pint milk

3 teaspoons each of cornstarch/cornflour, sugar and cocoa powder

1 ounce / 20 grams dark chocolate, broken into small pieces

2 tablespoons whipping/double cream

INGREDIENTS FOR THE DIPPERS (SELECT 2 OR 3)

slivers of sponge cake

chocolate-covered finger cookies/biscuits

small slices of brioche

fingers of cinnamon toast

Catch a Falling Star cookies/biscuits (see recipe on page 148).

INGREDIENTS FOR THE FLAVORINGS
(SELECT 4 OF THESE OR INVENT YOUR OWN!)

1 tablespoon Amaretto liqueur and 1 tablespoon toasted split almonds

2 pods of cardamom seeds, crushed

finely grated rind of one orange

1 ounce / 20 grams dark mint chocolate, finely chopped

1 tablespoon Bailey's liqueur

1 tablespoon chopped stem ginger with a little of its sugar syrup

Place the ramekins in an oven at 120F / 50C to warm up.

Assemble your flavorings and arrange the chosen dippers on a platter.

Blend the milk and the three powders in a food-processor, then pour this liquid into a saucepan. Slowly bring to a boil, stirring constantly. After 2 minutes of a gentle rolling boil, remove the pan from the heat and stir in the chocolate and cream.

Take the ramekins out of the oven and divide the hot mixture between them.

To each ramekin add one of the flavorings and stir. Arrange the ramekins on a platter with the dippers and serve.

Believe us, there are few more blissful communal dishes.

CATCH A FALLING STAR

These cookies are elevated far above their innate deliciousness by
their shape and sparkle. Fabulous on their own — especially pretty
when sandwiched together with raspberry ice cream.

2 cups / 225 grams all purpose/plain white flour

1/3 cup / 75 grams sugar

6½ ounces / 175 grams salted cold butter

3 tablespoons cold water

2 tablespoons powdered/icing sugar

1 teaspoon ground star-anise powder

2 tablespoons confectioner's glitter sugar*

star cutters

parchment/baking paper

Edible glitter can be bought from any good baking supplies store or directly from the internet. Three sites which sell it are: www.fancyflours.com, www.bakeitpretty.com, www.edible-glitter.co.uk.

Preheat oven to 350F / 180C.

Put the first 3 ingredients plus the star-anise powder into a food processor and process on slow until the mix starts to resemble breadcrumbs. This will only take about 20 seconds.

Add the cold water and mix again for a few seconds until the mixture binds together.

Wrap the dough in cling film and put in fridge to rest for at least 20 minutes. (You can leave for longer — even overnight — just remember to take out a few minutes before rolling so the mixture is not too hard.)

Dust your rolling pin with flour and roll out the dough to about 1/8-inch thick.

Cut stars with cookie cutter and place on baking tray covered with baking paper.

Cook for about 10 minutes or until barely golden.

Leave to cool while you make a paste with the icing sugar and a tablespoon of water.

Brush the paste onto cookies and sprinkle with the glitter sugar.

about us

WRITING DOWN THE VEIN OF GOLD

We are two good friends — one living alongside the lakes of northern England and the other on a sea-side mountain in Wales — whose friendship revolves around food. During the course of several meditation retreats (where doubtless we should have observed the silence a little more faithfully) we bonded through a common passion for cooking, for beauty, for Ladurée macaroons and for Paris. Our conversation grew through sharing favorite food writers, parties, shopping expeditions and Phillippa's catering business, which provided food for celebrations.

For both of us, the less tangible and more hidden dimensions of life are as fascinating and as real as what we see in front of us, and so it was natural that our interest extended to food in relation to spirituality. We started by writing small pieces about what currently most intrigued us, learning to use writing as exploration and research, delving deep into our memories and feelings and ranging broadly across what we saw in the culture around us. We experimented with recipes, seeking vibrant combinations which were as much fun to think about as to eat. We ran Kitchen Alchemy retreats, teaching people how to cook in creative, meditative and joyful ways and exploring healing issues concerning eating, weight and body image. Shopping in markets together, celebrating together during meals and our dialogue with retreat participants fed our writing in fresh ways.

Over twelve years (a real slow foodies movement!) we slowly pieced the writings together, many times looking afresh at the picture they created. This constantly changed, like a kaleidoscope, revealing more and more of what the book was about.

It was necessary to have long stretches of time to think and reflect, to connect with the concepts and their myriad ramifications, and then to pare down to their essence. This of course gave perfect opportunities to go and play in Scotland, in France and in remote areas of England, usually renting a house and shutting ourselves away from the rest of the world. The book became a wonderful vein of gold running through our lives as we followed the trail of the ideas in an organic and feminine way until we felt we were ready to have it go out into the world.

We continue to run cookery workshops and retreats in Spain and England, and the feedback we get shows us that there are many people out there who want to share these explorations with us and so to bring more love to bear upon the daily tasks of keeping body and soul together and of communing with each other through food. We welcome you to visit, explore and share with us at www.kitchenalchemy.org.

Phillippa Lee and Ann Bowen-Jones

Bouquets

We had never realised until writing *Kitchen Alchemy* what a total team effort birthing a book is, requiring midwives and doulas galore! First, to our publisher Victoria, thank you from the bottom of our hearts for believing in us and sending this book out into the world! To our editor Heather, you have seen right to the core of the message of this book, steadfastly probed, pruned and polished it until it shines, and we are profoundly grateful to you. Thomas, we adored seeing how you photographed the dishes and the kitchen shrines, with every little detail honored as heaven in a grain of sand — so much fun! Sandra, you have pulled the whole thing together so magnificently and brought the book truly alive. We are delightedly and gleefully grateful to you.

The prime role amongst our encouraging and patient-as-saints friends and family was played by Lynn Stuart. From the book's very conception, there she always was as cheerleader, grammar and syntax teacher, strength-giver, sense-maker, proof-reader and mopper-up of tears. Lynn, this book would not be here without you.

Peter, thank you for your support at all times in countless ways. You made it possible for me (Phillippa) to be free to write and play and I appreciate your continuing love.

Tom, thank you for believing in us and for the delight you gave us early on with the synopsis design. Great thanks also to the wonderful Renwick tribe, especially

Sue, Peter, Sophie and the black and white hen, for putting up with us, loaning us your house and views, and for always being there. And Nicky, thank you for your invaluable cooking skills and cheerfulness!

We are grateful also to all the participants in our cooking retreats for such stimulating discussions and so many memorably good times.

INDEX